EXOTIC TABLE

Flavors, Inspiration, and Recipes from Around the World—to Your Kitchen

ALIYA LEEKONG

Adamsmedia
AVON, MASSACHUSETTS

Published by
Adams Media, a division of F+W Media, Inc.
57 Littlefield Street, Avon, MA 02322. U.S.A.
www.adamsmedia.com

ISBN 10: 1-4405-5004-2
ISBN 13: 978-1-4405-5004-1
eISBN 10: 1-4405-5005-0
eISBN 13: 978-1-4405-5005-8

Printed in the United States of America.

10 9 8 7 6 5 4 3 2 1

Library of Congress Cataloging-in-Publication Data
LeeKong, Aliya.
 Exotic table : flavors, inspiration, and recipes from around the world - to your kitchen / Aliya LeeKong.
   pages cm
 Includes bibliographical references and index.
 ISBN-13: 978-1-4405-5004-1 (alkaline paper)
 ISBN-10: 1-4405-5004-2 (alkaline paper)
 ISBN-13: 978-1-4405-5005-8 (electronic)
 ISBN-10: 1-4405-5005-0 (electronic)
1. International cooking. I. Title.
 TX725.A1L36 2013
 641.59--dc23

2013015202

Always follow safety and commonsense cooking protocol while using kitchen utensils, operating ovens and stoves, and handling uncooked food. If children are assisting in the preparation of any recipe, they should always be supervised by an adult.

Eggs and nuts are used in a number of recipes described in this book. Infants, the elderly, pregnant, or breastfeeding women and persons who may otherwise be ill, are advised to avoid eating raw or lightly cooked eggs. Individuals with nut allergies should avoid eating peanuts and peanut products. Cooking time of meats should be calibrated to match the type of oven used and to ensure that they are properly cooked before serving to infants, the elderly, pregnant, or breastfeeding women and persons who may otherwise be ill. Efforts have been made in this book to identify recipes that contain gluten; however, individuals with a gluten allergy should examine each recipe carefully and consult their nutritionist as needed.

Many of the designations used by manufacturers and sellers to distinguish their product are claimed as trademarks. Where those designations appear in this book and F+W Media was aware of a trademark claim, the designations have been printed with initial capital letters.

Certain individuals may have been inadvertently captured in the scenery depicted in various photographs in this book. Where the author became aware of any potential infringement of any privacy or right to publicity of any such individuals, and it was possible to reach such individuals, efforts were made to obtain releases.

Photos by Aliya LeeKong. Photos of Aliya LeeKong by Michael Creagh.

Interior design by Elisabeth Lariviere.

This book is available at quantity discounts for bulk purchases. For information, please call 1-800-289-0963.

Brighter than fireflies upon the Uji River
Are your words in the dark, Beloved.
—AMY LOWELL

To the love of my life, Aren LeeKong.

Acknowledgments

Sewit Ahderom, Eman Al Rashed, Penelope Alzamora, Ayse, Bel Benedetti, Rajesh Bhardwaj, Francisco Klimscha Bittig, Andrew Blackmore, Naguib Ciurlizza, Michael Creagh, Jack Dancy, John Alfredo Davis, Walter D'Rozario, Yvette Dizon, Gerti Easterbrook, Emine and Emine, Sabita Fernandes, Raphael Francois, Benedict Hadley, Hawa Hassan, Raman Iyer, Wade Jackson, Eli Kaimeh, Irene LeeKong, Hibist Legesse, Rosemarie Lewis, Mama at Bati, Hemant Mathur, Nacho Miguel, Nick Miscusi, Angie Mitchell, Eric Murnighan, Aslihan Mutlu, Akhtar Nawab, Banu Ozden, Hamida Patel, Rameela and Salim Patel, Pepi and Manghala, Kristin Pernicano, Yahaira Rodriguez, Selin Rozanes, Carl Scott, Charlie Scott, Gwendolyn Scott, Fernando Silva, Nafisa and Aziz Tejpar, Rosy Tejpar, Don Tellock, Dwayne Alistair Thomas, Pio Vasquez de Velasco, Vincent from Montego Bay . . . and anyone else that I've missed here who invited me into their kitchens and helped me on my culinary path.

Thank you to all of the people that helped make this book possible. Their generosity to open their homes, hearts, and kitchens over the years allowed me to glimpse into their way of doing things and broaden the way that I do mine.

Contents

Introduction 9

Chapter 1: Spices, Ingredients, and Equipment 11

Homemade Pomegranate Molasses 19

Egyptian Dukkah 20

Harissa 21

STORY

My Personal Spice Trade 22

Merkén 24

Ras El Hanout 25

Sambal Oelek 25

Roasted Garlic 26

NOLA Creole Seasoning 26

Za'atar 27

West African Tsire 27

Spiced Honey 28

Chapter 2: Hors d'Oeuvres and Snacks 29

Harissa and Cheese–Stuffed Fried Olives 31

Peruvian Clams à la Parmesana 33

Exotic Cheese Crackers 37

STORY

Turkey's Culinary Crossroads 39

Heirloom Tomato Galettes with Urfa Chilies, Mint, and Ricotta Salata 41

Sugar and Spice Pecans 44

Deviled Eggs Three Ways: Indonesian, Greek, and Mexican 46

Red Lentil Pâté with Toasted Cashews and Indian Spices 49

Crispy Roasted Chickpeas with Merkén, Garlic, and Thyme 52

Smoky Eggplant Dip with Fingerling Chips . . .53

Homemade Popcorn with Spiced Honey and Butter 56

Chapter 3: Soups and Salads 57

Sopa de Flor de Calabaza (Squash Blossom Soup) 58

Harira 61

Trinidadian-Chinese Wonton Soup 63

Spiced Chestnut Soup 66

Lemon-Egg Soup with Quinoa 68

STORY

The Art of the Easy Homemade 70

Massaged Kale Salad with Pear, Fresh Cheese, and Pomegranate Vinaigrette 72

Israeli Couscous Salad with Lemon, Fennel, and Basil 75

Cucumber and Avocado Salad with Yuzu-Honey Dressing. 79

🌼 STORY
Peruvian Rhythms. 81

Peruvian Fava Bean and Corn Salad (Solterito) 83

Green Mango and Carrot Slaw with Fresh Chili, Peanuts, and Mint 85

Butter Lettuce Salad with Radish, Avocado, and Creamy Sesame-Buttermilk Dressing 86

Chapter 4: Fish and Seafood 87

Sautéed Rhode Island Calamari with Garlic, Cherry Peppers, and Bread Crumbs 89

🌼 STORY
Wandering Brazil 91

Mussels with African Chilies and Coconut (Moqueca-Style). 93

Charred Honey-Miso Smoked Salmon 96

Chicken Fried Scallops 98

Creole Shrimp and Grits 100

🌼 STORY
My Thanksgiving Mashup 102

Lobster Macaroni Pie with Bacon Bread Crumbs. 104

Crab Cakes with Mustard Seeds and Parsnips. 107

Salt-Baked Fish with Chermoula 109

Paella de Marisco 112

Tiradito with "Leche de Tigre" 116

Chapter 5: Poultry 117

Butterflied Za'atar Roast Chicken 118

Arroz Con Pato 122

Kenyan Coconut-Coriander Chicken 126

🌼 STORY
The Virtue of Fried Chicken. 128

Saffron Fried Chicken 131

Chicken Salad with Bacon, Walnuts, and Fruit 133

Korean-Style BBQ Chicken or Turkey Drumsticks. 135

"Chicken and Biscuits" 138

Baked Chicken with Chorizo, Fennel, and Green Olives. 142

🌼 STORY
Universal BBQ. 144

Jamaican Jerk Hens. 146

Moroccan Chicken Pie 149

Crispy, Brick Chicken Thighs with Roasted Garlic and Sweet Lemon-Ginger Confit. 151

Chapter 6: Beef, Pork, Lamb, and Goat 153

Espresso-Chipotle St. Louis–Style Spare Ribs. 154

Honey-Braised Lamb Shanks with
Butternut Squash and Apples 157

My Feijoada. 160

Cowboy Steak with Tellicherry Peppercorns
and Balsamic–Red Onion Marmalade. 162

🌸 STORY
How to Make Browning 165

Pappardelle with West Indian Stewed
Oxtail Ragu. 166

Pork Chops with West African Tsire
and Pan Gravy 169

Smoky Lamb Meatballs 172

Short Rib Chili with Ethiopian Spices 174

Roasted Marrow Bones with Garlic
and Herbed Bread Crumbs 176

🌸 STORY
A Lesson in South African Cookery . . . 179

South African Shepherd's Pie (Bobotie) 180

Rosy's Beef and Potato Patties 183

Goat Biryani 186

Greek Lasagna 190

Chapter 7: Vegetables and Side Dishes 193

Corn with Green Chili Butter
and Toasted Coconut. 194

Wild Mushroom Quinotto 197

Roasted Cauliflower with Bread Crumbs,
Saffron, and Dried Cranberries 199

Patatas Bravas–Inspired Salad 202

🌸 STORY
Importance of Ingredients. 204

Savory Winter Vegetable Crumble. 205

Smoky Corn Pudding with
Mustard Seeds and Curry Leaves 207

Garlicky Beet Greens with
Fish Sauce and Chili 210

🌸 STORY
Don't Let the Pepper Burst! 213

Gran's Peas and Rice 215

Summer Squash and Burst Cherry
Tomatoes with Brown Butter, Coriander,
and Hazelnuts 218

Chai-Spiced Sweet Potato Pie. 220

Cassava Fries with Chili-Lime Salt. 222

Chapter 8: Breakfast, Savory Tarts, and Breads 223

Shakshouka with Chorizo and
Bread Crumbs 224

Mexican Breakfast Quiche 228

Vanilla-Cinnamon Chia Pudding Parfait. . . . 230

Crab Kedgeree 232

🌸 STORY
*The Beauty of Sunday Cooking
and Eating* 234

East African Donuts (Mandazis) 236

Banana Chocolate Chip Muffins 238

Mushroom and Ajwain Pissaladière 240

Goat Cheese Tart with Mission Figs,
Pistachios, and Anise. 242

Guava and Cheese Danishes 245

Parker House Rolls with Sweet Miso Butter . . 247

Fried "PB&J's" 250

Chapter 9: Desserts 253

End-of-Summer Bread Pudding (of sorts). . . . 254

Persimmon Tarte Tatin 257

Mexican Chocolate Loaf Cake 260

Hot Coffee-Glazed Medjool Date Cakes 263

❀ STORY

Food Is Giving 266

Meyer Lemon Cream with
"Amarena-Style" Cherries 267

Salted Caramels with Sweet Garam Masala . . 270

❀ STORY

Grandmother's Tribute 272

Nani's Fruit Spice Cake 274

South African Milk Tart with Fruits 277

Espresso-Chocolate Brigadeiros 281

Hibiscus Paletas 284

Shrikhand with Strawberries and
Balsamic Caramel 286

Chapter 10: Drinks 289

Cape Gooseberry Sour 291

Melon Horchata 293

Frozen Limonada 295

Pink Grapefruit Paloma 296

St. Lucian Rum Punch. 298

Cherry-Yuzu Champagne Floaters 300

Thyme-Green Tea Cocktail 301

Black Plum and Hibiscus "Sangria" 304

❀ STORY

Kahawa in Dar Es Salaam 307

Kahawa na Tangawizi (Coffee with Ginger) . . 308

Standard U.S./Metric
Measurement Conversions 309

Index 310

Introduction

Over the years, I've noticed that when you talk to people about food, it's never *really* about the food. Sure, it starts that way. You discuss what someone likes to cook, ingredients that resonate, dishes their family loves, but then it almost always becomes a conversation about how they grew up, their childhood food memories, history, and strong life influences.

I, like many others, learned at my mother's and other family members' hips in the kitchen. My heritage is multicultural—Indo-Pakistani and Tanzanian—and I remember how both the cuisines and mother tongues of my parents blended as a child, to the extent that I was never quite sure to which side a particular dish or word belonged. This blend was completely natural, a personal mashup, and certainly has spilled over into my way of thinking about life and food.

The idea of making food based on your personal history is found in countries all over the world. After all, a country or region's cuisine is a direct reflection of its history— war, invasion, immigration of peoples. Each additional culture contributes bits and pieces along the way. For example, Peruvian culture is inclusive of the indigenous Native Americans, conquering Spanish (some with Arabic wives), and Japanese and Chinese immigrants. South Africa has Dutch, Malay, Indian, Arab, Portuguese, German, and the indigenous African tribes like Khoikhoi, Xhosa, and Zulu. Turkey's cuisine came from the Mongols, Chinese, Persians, European Mediterraneans, and other Arabic and Slavic influences. And I might even be *missing* some influences in these lists.

America is no different, and has certainly become one of the most open cultures, attempting to embrace diversity. Immigrants come from all over the world; families move and migrate and marry. I'm now married to a guy from Brooklyn, whose family comes from Trinidad by way of Venezuela, Spain, and China. What I cook at home is a complete amalgamation of both of our cultures' histories. Though many dishes are based in the past, I sometimes imagine our future children and the blend that they will grow up understanding as their own.

Many of us start off with culture that's passed on from our family, and then we build on it by absorbing aspects from our own life. That's what I like to call a person's *cultural layers*: family, education, marriage, travels, influences of friends and colleagues, likes, and dislikes. All of these factors play into the way a person cooks.

We are incredibly fortunate to live in a time when different ingredients and spices are readily accessible, and when other cultures' foods have comingled and entered the American dialogue. What might have been called *exotic* just ten years ago might not be so today.

I cook, quite simply, the way that I eat. My style is not about *elevation* or *modernism*; it's just my personal way of preserving food traditions. I am not a purist, and my travels, heritage, family, or even culinary training, serve merely as inspiration—I do not declare that anything I cook is exactly per the tradition. I work with what I can find, have on hand, or simply prefer flavorwise. I encourage you to follow the same idea as you read through my stories and try the recipes in this book.

Look for recipes where traditions, spices, or ingredients from other cultures make that easy transition into your own, when they become something translatable, taking foods you know and love to another level. For example, you could simply incorporate a new spice or blend into a recipe you have lying around, or you could try a technique you learned from another culture on an ingredient your family already likes.

Just like you, I go to the grocery store. I entertain for friends and family. I have busy weeknights. I have friends who are vegan, and some who are eating gluten-free. All of that is reflected in this book. (Look for the labels to show you which recipes are vegetarian, vegan, or gluten-free. In addition, consider that some recipes can be made vegetarian or vegan simply by swapping vegetable stock for chicken stock, for example.)

I take the idea of *exotic*, which is to say globally influenced through my personal lens, and bring it into my everyday cooking. I honor my American sensibilities and simultaneously pay homage to the flavors and traditions of a variety of ethnicities—this is my *Exotic Table*. I make things easier or simpler where it's efficient, but I'm also not afraid of the old-school: long braises, sauces from scratch, and a complex layering of flavors.

Food is subject to interpretation, to personal reinvention, and my goal is not to give you a set way of doing things. I'm a teach-a-woman-to-fish kind of gal, and food is ultimately about identity, a language containing your own heritage and traditions. Take my ideas and see how they work with your own cultural layers. Play, experiment, make them yours, and see what blend you come up with.

Chapter 1

SPICES, INGREDIENTS, AND EQUIPMENT

This next section is dedicated to what I like to call my Exotic Pantry—some of my favorite spice blends and condiments that I keep in my kitchen at all times. These are building blocks . . . truly easy ways to start creating your own layers of flavor.

Having these items at the ready means one less step and, for me, a more seamless and enjoyable cooking process. It's easy to jazz up everyday cooking when you have a little Ras El Hanout, a fragrant North African spice blend, or Sambal Oelek, a good, basic chili paste, around. You'll see that many of the recipes from other chapters of the book pull from this section, but my hope is that you come up with your own uses for them too.

Using whole spices and grinding them where I've noted creates incredible flavor—but if you only have ground spices on hand, start from there. Make these blends your own, tweak to your individual tastes, and work them into the dishes you love best.

Spices

Spices, to me, form a cuisine's signature—that aromatic blend that provides instant information as to a dish's origins. I keep my pantry stocked and go through a decent quantity of spices on a regular basis. As you decide which flavors you like best, you can do the same thing.

Keeping Spices Fresh

Here are a few keys to maintaining their intense flavor:

- Keep spices in airtight containers in a cool, dark spot away from humidity. Light, heat, and moisture all degrade the flavor. Ground spices stay fresh for 6 months, and whole spices up to a year.
- You can keep chili flakes in airtight containers at room temperature if they are of the drier sort. If the chili flakes are oily, like an Aleppo or Urfa chili, store them in the freezer. This helps their flavors stay bright and fruity, and they will keep for up to a year.
- Whole spices keep their flavor more intensely and for a longer period of time than ground spices because they have less surface area for the aroma and flavor to dissipate from. Try to grind spices in small quantities as you need them—I do this regularly with items like black pepper, cumin seeds, and cinnamon.
- Toasting spices can bring them back from the dead. If you taste a ground spice and there's no spark, try toasting it in a dry skillet over a medium-low flame to see if that revives the flavor.
- If you must keep a spice in ground form, try to keep it in a smaller quantity and buy it more often to make sure it's as fresh as possible.
- When using spices in a recipe, measure them out into a small bowl or your palm before approaching the stove in order to keep the container away from the steam and heat.

Commonly Used Spices In This Book

You can find many of the spices used in this book at your everyday grocery store, but you might need to look online or at an ethnic grocer in your area for some of the specialty spices.

SALT

Salt is mentioned first because it is the single *most* important spice you'll use. Salt is key to achieving depth of flavor; the rest of the spices and aromatics in a dish will have no meaning without it.

Salt is in nearly every recipe in this book, and in most places, unless otherwise specified, I use kosher salt. I find the flavor cleaner, and it absorbs quickly into dishes and has no additives. You'll also see flake salt, like Maldon, referred to throughout the book—this is beautiful as a finishing salt because the large flat crystals provide great texture to a dish. For my spice blend recipes in the book, I add salt in moderation. This allows you to use your own judgment when you are adding it to a dish—for example, to a stew with a salted broth or on meat versus fish—and to decide the right overall level for the dish.

OTHER SPICES

Ajwain seeds: You may have seen ajwain seeds labeled as ajowan, bishop's weed, or even carom seeds, and they're actually a member of the parsley family. The leaves are not really used in cooking, and the seeds bear a close resemblance to small cumin or celery seeds. The seeds contain high levels of thymol, the volatile oil in thyme, but they have a slight bitterness, even a sharp peppery bite, to them. Cooking them brings out the herbaceous quality in them and mellows most of the bitterness.

Aleppo chili flakes: Aleppo chilies come from Syria and are named after the northern city of Aleppo. This chili flake has often been compared to ancho and is fruity, moderately hot, with smoky undertones that come from being sun-dried. It has an acidic tartness to it and is actually a little salty; the heat hits fast and then subtly lingers. This is my favorite all-around chili flake for cooking because it has robust flavor and the perfect amount of heat.

Anardana: Anardana are pomegranate seeds that have been air-dried—a process that renders them caramelized and concentrated with pomegranate flavor. They are slightly sweet yet a bit sour. Look for a moister seed—if the seeds are dry and hard, it's a bad batch, and they just won't be as flavorful.

Berbere: Berbere is a key ingredient in Ethiopian cooking. It gives their stews that blood-red color and signature spiced flavor. Berbere comes in a ground form that's a complex blend of dried chilies, garlic, ginger, and red onion with such spices as fenugreek, ajwain, cardamom, cloves, cinnamon, cumin, nutmeg, black pepper, turmeric, and an herb called sacred basil.

Black pepper: Freshly ground black pepper shows beautifully in a dish. I personally prefer Tellicherry peppercorns, which come from their namesake region on India's Malabar coast. Versus other black peppercorns, this one is cleaned of stems and lesser quality peppercorns, and is extra large. It's largely regarded as the highest quality black peppercorn in the world and, with its high volatile oil content, has a strong fragrance and pungency. With Tellicherry pepper, a little goes a long way.

Cardamom: Cardamom comes in a pod form (white, green, and black) with the green version being the most readily available. It's known for having astringency and a warm, camphorous, palate-clearing flavor. Whereas green is more pungent and has a menthol flavor, black cardamom is earthier—less eucalyptus and more woodsy and smoky.

Chili powder: The chili powder I use throughout the book is a hot, Indian version. If you find that your chili powder lacks heat, feel free to supplement with cayenne.

Dill seeds: Dill seeds are flat, tear-shaped seeds and are actually the fruits of the dill plant. The flavor of the seed is stronger than the herb; it has a sharper bite and none of the leafy sweetness. For me, caraway is the closest taste comparison. Dill also contains notes of chervil, parsley, and anise, which isn't surprising since the plants are all in the same family. The seed definitely gets a boost from dry-roasting, but it should be ground to order, as the flavor dissipates quickly after being ground.

Fenugreek: Fenugreek seeds are small, hard, and rectangular and have a bitter, vegetal flavor. They also have maple syrup–like notes, particularly when toasted. The seeds are generally known to be used in Indian cooking and give curries their signature flavor.

Garam masala: Garam masala is a blend of spices used predominantly in Indian cooking and typically includes cumin, coriander, cardamom, peppercorns, cinnamon, clove, bay leaf, nutmeg, and ginger, though blends may vary.

Granulated garlic and granulated onion: I prefer granulated garlic and granulated onion over the traditional powder forms because I find the texture allows for easy mixing in rubs and marinades and it doesn't cake or clump up over time like the powder does. Granulated garlic also holds its flavor on the shelf for longer. If you only have powder on hand, cut back on the amount in the recipe by ⅓ to ½, depending on the potency.

Mustard seeds: Mustard seeds are the small black, brown, or yellow seeds of the mustard plant. They are bitter when raw, but mellow through cooking with a balanced, slightly hot,

mustard flavor. Most often, they are fried in hot oil until they pop to release their flavor.

Nigella seeds: Nigella seeds are tear-shaped, matte, and coal-black. They are bitter when raw, but when cooked, there develops a peppery, almost oregano-like flavor. The spice is often confused with black cumin or black sesame seeds, but the taste is vastly different from either of those.

Pimentón de La Vera (smoked Spanish paprika): For this paprika, Spanish peppers from the La Vera region are oakwood-smoked and dried before being milled. The result is a deep red, smoky spice with varying degrees of heat.

Saffron: Saffron threads are the stigmas from the crocus flower and are picked by hand. It's one of the most versatile spices, amazing in both savory and sweet dishes, and has a distinctive, floral aroma. I'm partial to Persian saffron—it has a lower moisture content, which means it keeps for a longer period of time and also crushes easily into a powder so you can use less.

Sumac: Sumac is a deep burgundy–colored spice powder made from crushed sumac berries. The flavor is tangy and pleasantly sour with fruity undertones. Sumac trees are found predominantly in the Mediterranean region and throughout the Middle East, and the spice is a staple in Middle Eastern cooking. It is used as a souring agent and is a key ingredient in za'atar.

Turmeric: Turmeric is a rhizome (or a root) that's typically boiled, dried, cleaned, and crushed into powder form to get the signature deep orange-yellow spice we're all used to seeing. The flavor is a bit bitter, earthy, and an aggregator—it helps meld together the aromatics like onion and garlic and the various spices in a dish.

Urfa chili flakes: Urfa chili flakes (biber) are made by coarse-grinding a pepper grown in southeastern Turkey, close to Syria. They range in color from burgundy to purplish-black and undergo a two-part process, alternatingly dried in the sun and wrapped overnight. This process develops the amazingly smoky, sweet, and earthy character. The flavor is a lot like ancho chilies, although with a bit more heat.

Fats

I'll disclaim here that I'm not a low-fat kind of gal. My personal preference is to eat a smaller quantity of more fully flavored (and full-fat) food than to snack away at empty calories. To that end, here are the main fats I use:

Butter: There is no getting around butter for flavor, and I use it where needed throughout this book. I strictly work with unsalted butter so that the salt can be controlled.

Oils: The oils I use the most are canola, olive, or a canola/olive blend. I find canola oil to be stable, with a high smoking point, and it's neutral enough to let spices and flavors shine through. Olive oil has a distinctive flavor, so for me, it works best with specific dishes. I use extra-virgin olive oil for salads and finishing only.

Ingredients

The ingredients from the dishes in this book span the globe but may also be found at your local farmers' market. Whenever possible, cook with peak-season fruits and vegetables to maximize flavor. Following are a few ingredients that you may or may not have seen. For the hard-to-find ones, I provide substitutes in the recipes themselves.

Cassava: Cassava is a thick, starchy root vegetable that's also known as *manioc* or *yuca*. It's a staple food in many parts of Africa and Latin America, and the flesh can become a bit sticky or gummy when cooked. The root should be firm to the touch and of an even color.

Chia seeds: The chia plant is a member of the mint family, native to parts of Mexico and Guatemala. The seed is a complete source of protein, has more calcium than skim milk on a per-ounce basis, and is the richest plant source of omega-3. In water, the seeds swell up and become gelatinous (like basil seeds), actually holding nine to twelve times their weight in water.

Chilies: I tend to work with fresh chilies rather than dried whenever possible. My favorites are Thai, serrano, Fresno, and jalapeño chilies (in order of decreasing heat). I use Scotch bonnets and habaneros for their intense flavor in a few recipes, but they are scorchingly hot. Make sure to wear protective gloves when chopping, and deseed and devein them before using.

Coconut milk: I have made my own coconut milk in the past, which provides the best flavor. You basically blend the flesh of a brown coconut with the coconut's water and a few cups of hot water. Strain and squeeze the grated coconut in batches with muslin to get the first milk. You can moisten the grated coconut and squeeze to get a second, thinner milk as well. The store-bought, canned version works fine for the recipes in this book, too.

Curry leaves: The fragrant curry leaf is found mostly in South Asian cooking. They get their name because of their use in curries, but the leaves can also be pan-roasted with a little oil to add flavor to a host of dry dishes. Curry leaves are woodsy, lemony, and actually a little smoky, with no curry flavor whatsoever. The leaf can be frozen for storage purposes, but it does lose some of its flavor that way.

Dutch process cocoa powder: Dutch process cocoa powder is natural cocoa powder that has been alkalized to neutralize its natural acidity.

Fruit molasses (pomegranate, grape, date, etc.): Historically, sugar was extraordinarily expensive in regions outside of India. During the summer months when sweet fruits were plentiful, the fresh juice of these fruits was boiled and reduced down to create intensely flavorful and perfectly sweet syrups, or molasses. These syrups were the ideal sweeteners, capitalizing on peak-season fruit, and were kept for months. In this book, I use these natural sweeteners and provide a recipe for how to make your own pomegranate molasses (see recipe in this chapter).

Guava paste (*Pasta de Guayaba* or *Goiabada*): Guava paste is guava purée that's been cooked down with sugar and a bit of pectin. It sets into a semisolid, gelatinous state and is used in Latin American cooking.

Hibiscus flowers (dried): Dried hibiscus flowers can often be found at tea shops, ethnic grocers, and specialty gourmet shops. The petals must be steeped in hot water to release their tart and floral flavor. They also go by the names *sorrel* and *flor de Jamaica*.

Medjool dates: Medjool dates are prized for being the largest and most flavorful of the date family. They have a tender, melt-in-your-mouth character and a flavor that is sweet with overtones of caramel and chocolate. A good date should be like dessert, albeit a bit healthier since it's high in fiber and minerals.

Mexican chocolate: Mexican chocolate is typically made with roasted cocoa nibs, sugar, and cinnamon, though it may include other spices or ingredients like chilies or nuts. It is found in bar form or in round, relatively flat disks. Mexican chocolate also refers to the hot drink made from the chocolate.

Mirin: Mirin is a distinctive Japanese rice wine, not unlike sake, and is found at many traditional grocers as well as Asian specialty stores.

Miso paste: Miso is a Japanese staple ingredient made from fermented soybeans, rice, or barley. I tend to use shiro miso, or white miso paste, which has a sweeter and more mellow flavor than the red kind.

Paella rice (Bomba and Callasparra): Paella rice is a shorter-grain, round rice that has a high starch content. It can absorb close to three times its volume in broth or water while still keeping its firm, structural integrity.

Palm sugar: Palm sugar is unrefined, naturally processed sugar cane, date palm, or even coconut palm sap. With less processing comes less depletion of vitamins and minerals, and a form of this unrefined, economical sugar is found in cuisines around the world, from South Asian to East Asian to West Indian and Latin American. The flavor is a combination of molasses, brown sugar, and butterscotch. It also has a low melting and high burning temperature, so it works well in everything from sauces to dry rubs.

Peruvian chilies: Peruvian chilies, or *ajis*, are extremely flavorful. Aji limo is long and red and used for garnishes and in ceviche. Aji amarillo is their yellow pepper, has a mild flavor, and is often used in paste form. Aji panca is usually found dried and has a flavor not unlike chipotle—sweet and a touch smoky. It's pretty difficult to find fresh versions of these chilies, but the jarred pastes are readily available online and at specialty grocers.

Stocks: Good stocks are a foundation in cooking. I use stocks throughout this book—for sauces, soups, and braises. Try making your own to achieve the greatest depth of flavor.

Orange blossom water: Orange blossom water comes from the blossoms of the Seville orange, a bitter and fragrant orange native to Asia. The petals of the flower are heated in water, and the resulting steam is condensed and separated, now scented with the orange blossom. The result is a clear liquid that is floral with orange citrus notes and a hint of bitterness. Having a light hand helps when it comes to this ingredient—it gets overwhelmingly perfume-y in excess. Be sure to taste your particular brand before following a recipe.

Yuzu: Yuzu is a Japanese citrus fruit with a highly aromatic and distinctive flavor. It contains notes of lime, grapefruit, and mandarin, a Meyer lemon–like sweetness, acidity, and, at the same time, it has a signature, aromatic, floral muskiness and salinity that I love.

Equipment

Here are some of my favorite kitchen tools and pots that can help you make the recipes in this book.

Cast-iron skillet: A good cast-iron skillet is a lifetime investment and is second only to the Dutch oven in my book. It's nonstick, has even heat distribution, and goes from stovetop to oven. You can use it for everything from shallow frying to baking pies to searing a steak.

Coffee grinder: This is my go-to device for grinding small portions of nuts and all of my spices. You can grind spices into a powdery texture with it, and it cleans up easily. Tip: Whir some salt in there every now and then to remove the lingering aromas.

Dutch oven: I can't live without my Dutch oven. Mine is cast-iron, provides really even and gentle heat, and holds the heat well. It's my go-to for one-pot meals, soups, stews, long braises, and even casseroles. The enameled versions are a bit more expensive, but worth it—they are nonreactive and so work well for tomato-based and other acidic dishes.

Ice cream scoop: Of course, it's fantastic for scooping ice cream, but I also use it to control size and portion. It's great for creating even amounts—batter for muffins, donuts, fritters, crab cakes, and biscuits, to name a few things.

Japanese mandoline: There's nothing better to quickly and evenly slice, julienne, or create even finer cuts for fruits and vegetables. Each piece looks the same and cooks evenly.

Potato ricer: This is *the* tool for creating beautiful, fluffy vegetable purées—mashed regular or sweet potatoes, parsnips, celery root, sunchokes, etc. I can't get through fall and winter without it.

Stand mixer: Although a hand mixer works pretty well for some recipes, you'll find using a stand mixer easier for others. It's great for cakes, cookies, dough, whipped cream, eggs, compound butters, and homemade marshmallows. If you have a few extra attachments, you can do everything from grind meat to make ice cream. This falls right after my cast-iron skillet in terms of utility in the kitchen.

Importance of Palate

The single most important tool? Your senses. Learning to trust your senses—sight, smell, and taste (even hearing and touch)—is an asset in the kitchen. It's what distinguishes a good cook from a great one!

Where to Buy

Following are some online resources for my favorite spices, ingredients, and kitchen tools.

Kalustyan's

Kalustyan's is my go-to global spice and "off the beaten path" ingredient megastore—I can peruse in there for hours and without fail walk out with something new to try. They have been around for decades, and their landmark store was where my mom used to get her spices when she lived in New York City in her early twenties. I buy a lot of my bulk spices here, know the quality is going to be incredible, and have even special-ordered hard-to-find items for restaurants in which I've worked. For me, wandering their physical store brings a great deal of joy, but they have pretty much everything online for order as well.

What they have: Aleppo or Urfa chili flakes, various fruit molasses, palm sugar, Peruvian chili pastes, Medjool dates, dried hibiscus flowers
Website: *www.kalustyans.com*

Penzeys Spices

Penzeys is another trusted source I use for single-note spices. Their quality is excellent, and they have a great range of spices to choose from.

What they have: Sumac, nigella seeds, smoked Spanish paprika
Website: *www.penzeys.com*

Zingerman's

Zingerman's is a fantastic resource for mail-order foodstuffs—everything from Italian wild cherries to specialty breads to gorgeous gift baskets for culinary enthusiasts. They also have great, high-quality ingredients I love to keep around my kitchen.

What they have: Harissa, stone-ground grits, Bomba rice, Mexican chocolate
Website: *www.zingermans.com*

Murray's Cheese

Whenever I plan to entertain, be it for a few friends or a full dinner party, I always stop by Murray's Cheese. They have a huge selection of gorgeous cheeses and charcuterie, and the staff is really knowledgeable. I also love the olive oils, vinegars, honeys, and preserves they have on hand . . . and can't help but splurge on my favorite Vermont Creamery cultured butter.

What they have: Every type of cheese you could want, cultured butter, extra-virgin olive oils, beautiful honeys
Website: *www.murrayscheese.com*

D'artagnan

I'm a big fan of D'artagnan and have cooked their heritage turkeys for Thanksgiving and bone-in short ribs for Christmas. They are an amazing source for fresh and cured meats, sausages, and gourmet specialty items.

What they have: andouille sausage, smoked duck and chicken breasts, demi glace
Website: *www.dartagnan.com*

Amazon.com

I am always shocked by what I can find on Amazon. There is literally no end—from spices to ingredients to equipment.

What they have: Ethiopian berbere, guava paste, Japanese mandoline
Website: *www.amazon.com*

Broadway Panhandler

This store is a cook's dream. From cookware to Japanese knives to baking supplies, they have it all.

What they have: Dutch oven, potato ricer, stand mixer
Website: *www.broadwaypanhandler.com*

Exotic Pantry
Homemade Pomegranate Molasses

Fruit molasses are eaten throughout the Middle East and Mediterranean and were an early and cheap sweetener when sugar was really expensive. In the West, we think of molasses as the super thick byproduct of the sugar process, but in these other parts of the world, fruit molasses is simply a cooking down of the must or juices of fruit until it turns to syrup. Pomegranate molasses is gaining in popularity but is not always the easiest to find. Cooking down 100% pomegranate juice gets you to the same place, so check out this homemade version of this delicious ingredient. VEGAN, GLUTEN-FREE

YIELDS APPROXIMATELY 1 CUP

48 fluid ounces pomegranate juice (100% juice like POM)

1. Pour the pomegranate juice into a medium saucepan and set over medium-high heat. Bring up to a boil and lower to a simmer. Simmer uncovered for 1 hour or until the juice is reduced to a syrup and coats a spoon.
2. The pomegranate molasses will still seem loose when it's hot but will thicken and become more of a syrupy texture as it cools.
3. Cool completely and keep refrigerated. This should keep for about 3 weeks to a month in the fridge.

This method should work with other juices as well—grape, blueberry, and cherry, to name a few. The cook time will differ for each depending on the sugar content, so just keep an eye out. Stick with 100% juice with no added sugars to keep it healthy.

Egyptian Dukkah

Egyptian dukkah is a warm spice blend that is eaten in Egyptian culture much like Za'atar (see recipe in this chapter) is in other ones, with bread and a little olive oil. Dukkah is another one of those recipes that differs from family to family. What stays constant is a base of roasted nuts—usually hazelnuts but sometimes pistachios, almonds, or cashews— and some combination of spices and herbs. My personal favorite ways to use this are on top of a mixed green or kale salad with some fresh cheese, sprinkled on roasted squash with shaved Grana Padano, or to finish up a nice seared or oven-roasted piece of fish. Nutty with a fragrant blend of spices, a tiny bit of heat, and that earthy mint . . . . Enjoy! VEGAN, GLUTEN-FREE

YIELDS APPROXIMATELY 1½ CUPS

¼ cup chopped hazelnuts
¼ cup chopped pistachios
½ cup white sesame seeds
¼ cup coriander seeds
2 tablespoons white cumin seeds
2 tablespoons fennel seeds
2 tablespoons dried mint
pinch chili powder
½ teaspoon black pepper
1½ teaspoons salt

1. Preheat the oven to 350°F. (As opposed to toasting in a skillet, I like to toast this blend up in the oven so the nuts and spices toast evenly.)

2. Line a baking sheet with parchment paper. Add the hazelnuts, pistachios, and all of the seeds and make sure they are in a single layer. Toast for 8 to 10 minutes—you should smell a really nutty fragrance.

3. Transfer toasted nuts and spices to a mortar and pestle or a spice/coffee grinder. I like a slightly rough texture for this, so grind until there are still bits and pieces and it's not completely powder.

4. Combine with the dried mint, chili powder, black pepper, and salt. Store in an airtight container, preferably in a cool spot—it will keep for about a month.

> Toasting spices accomplishes a number of things—it coaxes out the aromas in the spice while simultaneously mellowing out the flavor a bit. It also brings out a nuttiness that adds great complexity to a blend or a dish.

Harissa

Harissa is a hot chili paste that is a staple in North African cuisines, especially in Tunisian and Algerian foods. Just like recipes in other cultures, harissa ingredients vary from household to household and region to region—some include cumin, others tomatoes, and even rose petals. In Tunisia, harissa is served with every meal—as a condiment, rubbed on meats, incorporated into stews, and mixed in with couscous. Tunisians use Nabeul and Gabes peppers, which are hotter but similar in flavor to readily available Anaheim and Guajillo chilies here in the States. This recipe is for a milder harissa because I like to control my heat, but you can make this harissa as spicy as you want using hotter dried chilies! VEGAN, GLUTEN-FREE

YIELDS APPROXIMATELY ½ CUP

3 medium New Mexican or Anaheim dried red chilies
4 medium Guajillo chilies
2 teaspoons Urfa or other chili flakes
1 teaspoon caraway seeds
½ teaspoon fennel seeds
pinch saffron (optional)
1½ teaspoons ground coriander
½ teaspoon turmeric
1 teaspoon salt plus more, to taste
2 sundried tomatoes (packed in oil or rehydrated)
2 garlic cloves
olive oil, to form paste and cover
freshly squeezed lemon juice, to taste

1. Remove seeds and ribs from the dried chilies and place in a heat-safe bowl. I like to use kitchen scissors for this—it's easy to just split them open, brush out the seeds, and pull out the ribs. Pour boiling water over chilies and let them soak 15 to 20 minutes until softened.

My Personal Spice Trade

I am generally a law-abiding citizen and grew up with a strong sense of right and wrong. But when it comes to my personal spice-smuggling, that all goes out the window. One of the highlights of literally every trip I take is the spice (or utensil or ingredient) stash with which I walk away.

On a ladies' trip with my mom to Dubai, I stuffed Emirati *bzar*, a blend of countless spices including cumin, coriander, fenugreek, and cardamom and a key ingredient in the region's stews and rice dishes, into a sock and carefully placed it under layers of other clothes. In Goa, a trip to a spice farm turned me into a hoarder, and I grabbed as many individual spices as I could—fresh cloves, massive cinnamon sticks, bright green cardamom, shiny brown nutmeg (to name a few)—all packed in flimsy plastic bags. Needless to say, my clothes paid the price on that one. In Paris, it's always teas, Herbes de Provence, and an idiotic number of different mustards.

I've nabbed a brass samovar and beautiful little coffee cups from Marrakech, a stone spice grinder from Cusco (that must have weighed 30 pounds), and a coconut grater that you have to sit on to use (okay, this one raised an eyebrow from my husband as if to say "are you *really* going to do that?"). A spoon here, a bowl there . . . .

I can't resist it! It's the packaging, the allure, the reminder of the locale . . . and the reality is, when it comes to spices, the closer to the source, the more intense and fresh they are, and I can never turn my back on the bright yellow pop of turmeric or the fresh red color of mace.

And why *should* I declare these items? They are mine. My little find. My secret pinch. And border control cannot tell me otherwise . . . .

2. You can do this in either a food processor or a blender. If you are doing this in the food processor, use a spice grinder to grind the chili flakes, caraway seeds, fennel seeds, and saffron first before adding those to the food processor. If working with a blender, add those ingredients first and blend until ground before moving on to the next step—it's like one big spice grinder.

3. Add ground coriander, turmeric, salt, sun-dried tomatoes, and garlic cloves. Remove chilies from water and wring out any excess moisture. Add to the blender or food processor. Pulse adding olive oil, 1 tablespoon at a time, until a thick paste is achieved and all the chilies have been ground up. Add lemon juice to taste and adjust seasoning as necessary.

4. Transfer to a jar and cover harissa with a layer of olive oil to preserve it. Keep refrigerated. It will keep for up to a month in the fridge.

Merkén

Merkén is like Chilean adobo—an all-purpose seasoning that's used throughout the country's hearty stews, soups, and even salsas—and is a key part of the cuisine of the Mapuche (an indigenous tribe). It has a smoky aroma with a touch of heat and citrusy notes from the coriander. Some versions include cumin seeds, but I personally prefer mine without. This is an incredibly versatile blend, and I use it in lieu of chili powder or paprika in many recipes. This blend definitely has a bit of heat, but you can reduce the level by discarding the seeds from inside the dried chilies. VEGAN, GLUTEN-FREE

YIELDS APPROXIMATELY 1 CUP

6 dried ancho chilies
6 dried red chipotle chilies
scant ½ cup whole coriander
1½ teaspoons salt

1. Heat a large skillet over medium heat. Add chilies and toast for 3 to 4 minutes. Remove the chilies from the pan. Add the coriander to the skillet and toast for 3 to 4 minutes, until fragrant, and then transfer to a bowl.

2. Using scissors, hold the chilies over the bowl with the coriander, cut the stem end, and discard. Then, cut the chilies into ½" pieces.

3. Add the salt to the chilies and coriander and transfer mixture to a mortar and pestle or a spice grinder. You can do it by hand if you like to create a great texture or simply whir it in the spice grinder (working in batches).

4. Store in an airtight container in a cool spot—it should keep for up to 3 months.

Ras El Hanout

This North African blend is another staple I always have on hand in my exotic pantry. Ras El Hanout quite literally means "top of the shop" and is supposed to represent the most coveted blend the spice merchant has to offer, but I like to think of it as a Moroccan curry. The flavor is nuanced and complex, a heady mixture that's difficult to describe. It tastes to me like the smell of walking into a spice shop! My shortened blend is an easy one and is great on weeknight chicken thighs, to jazz up some plain rice, or on roasted potatoes. VEGAN

There are countless variations of this North African specialty and each shop, family, and region has its own list of ingredients, sometimes reaching upwards of 40 spices! Rosebuds may be added for a floral touch, grains of paradise for a peppery note, lavender for aromatic purposes. Some spice merchants go so far as to add spices, herbs, or other extractions that have aphrodisiacal effects . . . clearly trying to get repeat customers!

YIELDS 1 SCANT CUP

¼ cup white cumin seeds
¼ cup sweet paprika
¼ cup ground black pepper
1 tablespoon ground cinnamon
2 teaspoons ground ginger
1½ teaspoons turmeric
1 teaspoon cayenne pepper
large pinch saffron
1 teaspoon salt

1. In a small skillet, toast cumin seeds over medium heat until they deepen in color and turn fragrant, about 3 to 5 minutes. Grind to a fine powder using a spice or coffee grinder.
2. Combine the ground, roasted cumin with the remaining ingredients.
3. Store in an airtight container—the blend should keep up to 3 months.

Sambal Oelek

I love sambal oelek because of just how basic it is. It's a chili paste, pure and simple, with hints of sweetness and a little bite of acidity. It originated in Southeast Asia along with a ton of other sambals. It's unadulterated, so when you add it to a dish, you can control the other aromatic flavors like onion and garlic that are often found in a chili sauce. Finger chilies give a great flavor here, but I've used Fresnos and loved it too. Although it's traditionally hand ground with a mortar and pestle, I use a food processor for convenience. VEGAN, GLUTEN-FREE

¾ pound red finger chilies (16–18 chilies)
2½ teaspoons salt
1 tablespoon palm or brown sugar
juice of 1 lime

1. Halve chilies and remove the seeds. Add to the bowl of a food processor along with salt and sugar and process until almost puréed.
2. Heat a pan over medium heat. Add puréed chili mixture and cook for 3 to 4 minutes, until thickened and some of the moisture has evaporated. Remove from heat and add lime juice.
3. Cool completely and store in an airtight container in the refrigerator. The sambal should keep for 1 to 2 weeks in the fridge.

Roasted Garlic

If you ever take a peek inside my fridge, you will always see some roasted garlic lying around. I love to add and deepen flavor at each step of my cooking, and roasting garlic is such a simple technique to extract beautifully caramelized flavor. You can substitute roasted garlic for raw garlic in so many different recipes—a compound butter for steak, pasta, my baked clams (see Chapter 2), vinaigrette— and you will love the difference it makes!

VEGAN, GLUTEN-FREE

4–6 heads of garlic
olive oil, to coat
salt and freshly ground black pepper, to taste

1. Preheat oven to 400°F.
2. Peel off the outer skins of the garlic and expose all layers of the garlic. Cut ¼" off the top of the garlic. This will help the roasted garlic cloves come out more easily.
3. Drizzle olive oil all over the exposed cloves and the skin and season with salt and freshly ground black pepper. Wrap each head in foil and place directly into the oven. Roast for 1 hour.
4. Pop the roasted cloves out and use as is or purée.

NOLA Creole Seasoning

This is a great all-purpose blend I learned down in New Orleans. I use it to flavor Creole dishes like shrimp étouffée, gumbos, and jambalaya, but this is also great as a dry rub on chicken or for simple, blackened fish. VEGAN, GLUTEN-FREE

YIELDS A LITTLE MORE THAN A CUP

2 tablespoons granulated garlic
2 tablespoons sweet paprika
1 tablespoon granulated onion
1 tablespoon dried oregano leaves
1 tablespoon dried thyme leaves
2 teaspoons dried sweet basil
1½ teaspoons ground black pepper
1½ teaspoons ground white pepper
1½ teaspoons celery seed
1½ teaspoons ground mustard
1½ teaspoons salt
¾ teaspoon cayenne pepper (or whatever you can stand!)

1. Mix all ingredients together.
2. Store in an airtight container—it should keep for about 3 to 6 months.

Za'atar

Over the last few years, za'atar has become my universal spice. Invariably, I have some stashed in my kitchen, and I break it out to flavor everything from homemade popcorn (I know, trés gourmet . . .) to killer roasted garlic bread (see Roasted Garlic recipe in this chapter) to a simple, weeknight roast chicken (see Chapter 5). The flavor is earthy with a nutty bite from the sesame seeds and a touch of tartness from the sumac. *This versatile spice is a staple of my exotic pantry.* VEGAN, GLUTEN-FREE

YIELDS 2½ CUPS

½ cup white sesame seeds
½ cup black sesame seeds
1 cup dried thyme
⅓ cup sumac
3 tablespoons salt

1. In a large skillet, toast white and black sesame seeds over medium-low heat until white seeds turn golden and the mix becomes fragrant.
2. Place in a bowl and add the dried thyme, sumac, and salt.
3. Mix thoroughly and store in an airtight container in a cool spot. The za'atar will keep for up to 3 months.

West African Tsire

West African Tsire powder is a spice blend of, traditionally, roasted peanuts with aromatic spices. I like to grind cashews in my blend because of the flavor, but feel free to use either. VEGAN, GLUTEN-FREE

YIELDS APPROXIMATELY 2½ CUPS

2 cups roasted, unsalted cashews (or traditional peanuts)
3 teaspoons mild chili powder
1 teaspoon ground cinnamon

½ teaspoon ground ginger
½ teaspoon ground nutmeg
½ teaspoon salt
¼ teaspoon allspice

1. In a small food processor or a coffee grinder, process the cashews until they're a powder. Be careful, as the machine heats up so will the cashews, and powder can quickly turn to "paste" from the release of the oils in the nuts. I like to work in batches to minimize this, and also pause and let the machine cool down if I need to.
2. Combine powdered cashews with remaining ingredients and store in an airtight container for 2 to 3 weeks.

Spiced Honey

With a few key spices, a simple ingredient like honey can go from sweet to savory and complex. I love to infuse honey with herbs and spices, and this infusion is easy and versatile. The garlic and onion add a great baseline taste; the toasted coriander adds nuttiness and an almost citrus-like quality; and the chili flakes add fruitiness and heat. I drizzle this hot over fried chicken, on triple-crèmes and crackers, or even on a simple turkey and Brie sandwich.

VEGETARIAN, GLUTEN-FREE

YIELDS APPROXIMATELY ½ CUP

½ cup honey
½ teaspoon salt

½ teaspoon granulated garlic
½ teaspoon granulated onion
½ teaspoon toasted coriander seeds, roughly crushed
¼ teaspoon Aleppo or other chili flakes

1. Add all ingredients to a small saucepan and bring up to a strong simmer. Reduce heat to very low and warm for about 10 to 15 minutes to let the flavors infuse.
2. Can be served hot or at room temperature. Store in an airtight container at room temperature—the spiced honey should last for about a year.

Chapter 2

HORS D'OEUVRES
AND SNACKS

The recipes in this section are designed with a dinner or cocktail party in mind. I frequently entertain, and you want items that are light and easy to handle while standing and mingling. They should whet the palate and keep your guests hungry for more.

Many of the recipes in this section, like the Sugar and Spice Pecans, Exotic Cheese Crackers, and the Crispy Roasted Chickpeas with Merkén, are nibbles, to be set down in proximity to a great cheese plate. Others are a bit more substantive and can be passed around or even set out together to create an appetizer spread—like the Heirloom Tomato Galettes with Urfa Chilies and the Deviled Eggs Three Ways. Still others can be whipped up quickly on a weeknight to calm a hungry household while you focus on the main meal.

None of these recipes are overly involved or require long, drawn-out techniques. When you're having a dinner party, you should be focused on your guests and not fussing with the food (at least that's what I tell myself!).

29

Harissa and Cheese–Stuffed Fried Olives

Fried olives may have originated in the Le Marche region of eastern Italy in a dish called Olives all'Ascolana. I wanted to experiment with some North African–flavored fried olives, so I stuffed them with a spicy, harissa-spiked cream cheese before rolling them in bread crumbs laced with freshly grated Parmigiano-Reggiano. A bit of tang from the cream cheese, some fiery heat from harissa, a touch of sweetness from honey—the briny olives become even more complex and have a deeply satisfying, deep-fried crunch. If you have never tried fried olives, now is your chance. VEGETARIAN

YIELDS 50 FRIED OLIVES

2 tablespoons ricotta cheese, room temperature

2 tablespoons cream cheese, room temperature

2 tablespoons harissa (see sidebar)

2 teaspoons honey

50 large pitted green olives, rinsed and thoroughly dried (you might try Castelvetrano, Cerignola, or Manzanilla olives)

½ cup panko or plain bread crumbs

¼ cup freshly grated Parmigiano-Reggiano

¼ cup all-purpose flour

1 egg, beaten

canola oil, for frying

fleur de sel

1. In a bowl, mix together ricotta, cream cheese, harissa, and honey until a uniform consistency. Transfer to a pastry bag fitted with the smallest pastry tip you have. (You can also use a Ziploc bag to do this—simply use scissors to cut off a small piece of the corner of the bag.) Pipe filling into all of the olives.

2. Set up a dredging station. Mix together the bread crumbs and Parmigiano-Reggiano in one bowl. Place the flour in another and the beaten egg in between. Roll the olives in the flour and dust off any excess. Dip into the egg and then roll in the bread crumb mixture until all are coated.

3. In a Dutch oven or pot, heat 2" to 3" of oil to 350°F. Carefully, drop olives into the oil, working in batches depending on the size of your vessel. Fry until a deep golden brown and remove to a paper towel–lined plate. If the olives are not too salty, sprinkle with a little fleur de sel.

4. Let cool slightly before serving. I love to line these up on a platter skewered with bamboo skewers with twisted ends.

For harissa, you can use my homemade version in Chapter 1 or the store-bought kind. Feel free to adjust the amount to your heat tolerance depending on the type of harissa you end up using.

Peruvian Clams à la Parmesana

While I was in Lima, I learned how to make conchitas a la parmesana, which are scallops on the half shell with aji amarillo, buttery Parmesan, and bread crumbs. When I came back, I thought local, littleneck clams would make the perfect substitute, and these little guys have quickly moved into my favorite spot for an easy and light hors d'oeuvre. Tasty and addictive, you can prep these ahead of time and throw them under the broiler for a few minutes once guests arrive. I use Pisco here, which is a grape brandy popular in both Peru and Chile, but tequila, a little whiskey, or even white wine would produce equally delicious results.

YIELDS 2 DOZEN CLAMS

coarse rock salt for baking

2 dozen medium littleneck clams, shucked with half shells reserved

1 tablespoon aji amarillo or other chili paste

2–3 tablespoons Pisco liqueur

¾ teaspoon Roasted Garlic purée (see Chapter 1)

¼ cup panko or plain bread crumbs

¼ cup freshly grated Parmigiano-Reggiano

3 tablespoons unsalted butter, melted

salt, to taste

chives, thinly sliced, for garnish

1. Preheat the broiler to high and place the rack in your oven on the second highest rack.

2. On one large baking sheet or two small ones, make a layer of rock salt as a bed and lay the half clamshells on top of the rock salt in a single layer. Place one clam inside each half shell. Place ⅛ teaspoon of the aji amarillo paste and a few drops of Pisco liqueur on each clam.

3. In a medium bowl, mix together the Roasted Garlic purée with the bread crumbs, Parmigiano-Reggiano, and melted butter. Salt to taste.

4. Place 1 to 2 teaspoons of the bread crumb mixture on each clam and place clams under the broiler. Broil for 3 minutes.

5. Let cool slightly before serving and garnish with the thinly sliced chives. I usually give guests a toothpick or small fork to eat these.

Aji amarillo chilies are native to South America and are used widely in Peruvian cuisine. Although they are often referred to as "yellow" chilies, their color is more of a bright orange, and the flavor is sweet and fruity with a fair amount of kick. Although they are difficult to find fresh in the United States, many Latin and gourmet grocers carry a paste of the chilies. If you can't find this paste easily, you can substitute your favorite type of chili paste or make your own by blending your favorite chili with just enough water to make the blade move.

Exotic Cheese Crackers

Ever try making homemade versions of grocery store favorites? These cheese crackers taste better than what you'll find in the snack aisle, and best of all, you get to control all of the (natural) ingredients that go into them. I make a big batch of these, freeze them precut and unbaked, and then freshly bake them when my friends come by. They work great for parties, by themselves, or even with a dip or topping as a passed hors d'oeuvre. Enjoy! VEGETARIAN

EACH VERSION YIELDS APPROXIMATELY 6 DOZEN CRACKERS

For the cracker base:

1 cup all-purpose flour

¾ teaspoon salt

½ stick cold, unsalted butter, cut into small cubes

3–4 tablespoons water

For Cheddar-Parm Crackers with Ajwain and Truffle Oil:

½ teaspoon ajwain seeds

½ teaspoon ground black pepper

4 ounces grated Cheddar cheese

4 ounces grated Parmesan cheese

1 teaspoon truffle oil

For Manchego Cheese Crackers with Anardana:

1½ teaspoons anardana (see sidebar)

8 ounces shredded manchego cheese

For Pepper Jack Crackers with Garlic and Herbs:

¾ teaspoon granulated garlic

¾ teaspoon granulated onion

½ teaspoon ground black pepper

¼ teaspoon dried thyme

¼ teaspoon dried oregano

8 ounces grated pepper jack cheese

1. Preheat oven to 350°F.

2. All of the crackers start with the same base. To the bowl of a food processor, add the flour, salt, and cold butter and pulse until the texture resembles a coarse meal. (You'll add the water at the end.)

3. Depending on which cracker option you are making, add the spices and cheese and pulse until combined. If you are making the Cheddar-Parm crackers, add in the truffle oil at this point as well.

4. Now, pulse in the water, one tablespoon at a time, until the dough comes together. You may not need the full 4 tablespoons, so watch the dough. It should be moist enough to press together and hold but not wet or sticky. Remove, wrap in plastic, and refrigerate for a minimum of 30 minutes.

5. Using parchment paper on either side, roll the dough out to ⅛" thickness and use a 1¼" cookie cutter to cut out crackers in your desired shapes.

6. Bake on a parchment-lined baking sheet for 15 to 20 minutes or until crackers are golden brown.

Anardana are pomegranate seeds that have been air-dried. They're found in the spice aisle of many Middle Eastern and South Asian grocers. If you can't find them, try substituting some dried currants; chop them up a bit before adding to the dough.

Turkey's Culinary Crossroads

When I'm travelling to learn about food, I look for a good cultural crossroads—that place where different people, languages, religions, and food traditions all intersect. Turkey was always on my shortlist of culinary destinations because of just how diverse, interesting, and deep its culture and its *food* culture are. Whether I was exploring a cave-like monastery, checking out a mosque that was once a church, trolling a market on the Asian side of Istanbul, or learning how to make *dolmas* from a Sephardic Jew in Nisantasi, Turkey did not disappoint, and the days never ceased to present the unexpected, food or otherwise.

Artisans are still treasured in Turkey, and tasting their cave-aged cheeses, oil-cured olives or pickle juice, and exploring the offal markets painted the picture of a people that care deeply about food and their traditions. In Kadiköy market in Istanbul, a cobblestone path was lined with stores full of dried fruits and nuts and tons of produce grocers showing off their quince and vine leaves. The fish stands with all the bright-red fish gills out smelled shockingly fresh! I even tasted a stuffed mussel on the street from the same store that sold me their gorgeous, in-house cured meats: pastirma and sujuk.

Much like the *appellation d'origine contrôlée*, the French system for certifying French products, Turks too are vigilant of the various regions from which they procure ingredients or other foodstuffs and what differentiates them. Vine leaves from Tokat are supposed to be the best, and their *biber* (peppers or chili flakes) differ across regions; the ones from Urfa I use in Heirloom Tomato Galettes with Urfa Chilies, Mint, and Ricotta Salata happen to be one of my personal favorites.

Learning cool bread-baking techniques in Ibrahimpasa village, I was shocked to see a *tawa* and a *tandoor*, what I was raised to believe were traditional South Asian cooking elements used to make breads. The Turks *did* invade India centuries ago, so it must have been cross-pollination.

Turkey was a wonderful stop on my own journey, and if Turkey validated one thing, it's that it's okay to break the rules a bit. The diversity and the mixing of cultures have created something strong and unique, a bit of revised tradition. The food is part Middle Eastern, part Eastern European, and part Central Asian . . . yet it works! It's beautiful, flavorful, and rooted, and I am ridiculously appreciative of all the folks who took the time to share their traditions with me.

Heirloom Tomato Galettes with Urfa Chilies, Mint, and Ricotta Salata

Turkish pide is the inspiration for this savory tart. The traditional dish is often referred to as Turkish pizza, a piece of yeast-based dough that is baked with various toppings—ground meat, tomatoes, and cheese—and folded over. I decided to lighten it up a bit and went with little savory galettes (flat, round pastry cakes), bringing in seasonal heirloom cherry tomatoes and some of those classic flavors of dried mint and chili flakes and finishing it with a little crumbled ricotta salata for a nice salty, nutty bite. These are fabulous as hors d'oeuvres or just a snack. Any way I can sneak in a pizza-esque dish, I do! VEGETARIAN

YIELDS APPROXIMATELY 10–12 GALETTES

1 pound heirloom cherry tomatoes, sliced thinly

1 sheet puff pastry, thawed according to package directions

2¼ teaspoons dried mint

¾ teaspoon Urfa chili flakes or other red chili flakes

salt and freshly ground black pepper, to taste

1 egg, beaten with a splash of cream or water

¼ cup ricotta salata, finely crumbled

1. Preheat the oven to 375°F.

2. Place the cherry tomato slices on paper towels and blot so they're as dry as possible. Place the puff pastry on a lightly floured work surface and roll out gently. You just want to straighten it out and get an even thickness, so don't roll it to be too thin. Using a 4½" round pastry cutter (or ramekin or jar mouth), cut 10 to 12 circles out of the puff pastry.

3. On each puff pastry round, overlap tomato slices in the center of each pastry, leaving a ½" rim. Sprinkle tomatoes generously with mint, chili flakes, salt, and freshly ground black pepper. Fold the edges of the pastry up over part of the tomatoes to form a ½" border, pleating as you go, and then brush the edges of the dough with egg wash.

4. Place galettes on a lightly greased baking sheet and bake for 25 to 30 minutes, until the crust turns golden brown and the tomatoes are cooked. Sprinkle with crumbled ricotta salata and serve warm or at room temperature.

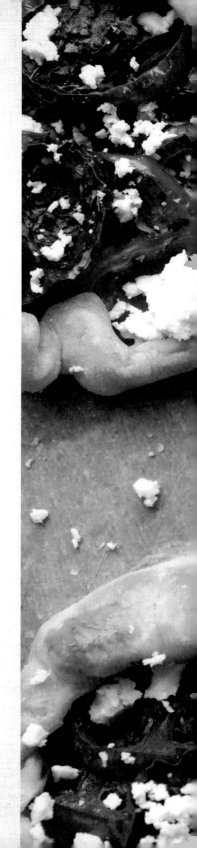

Sugar and Spice Pecans

These party snacks whip up in no time—toasted pecans, lightly caramelized and scented with a beautiful North African spice blend. I put these out next to my cheese plate and watch as they get inhaled. They have just the right touch of sweetness balanced with a salty, buttery warm spiciness that is irresistible. The best part? The leftover pecans can easily be tossed into a simple salad to dress it right up.

VEGETARIAN, GLUTEN-FREE

YIELDS APPROXIMATELY 4 CUPS

4 tablespoons unsalted butter

¼ cup honey

4 teaspoons light brown sugar

2 tablespoons Ras El Hanout (see Chapter 1)

1 teaspoon salt

1 pound pecan halves

1. Preheat the oven to 300°F.

2. In a skillet, melt the butter with the honey, sugar, Ras El Hanout, and salt over medium-low heat, whisking to dissolve the spices. Once it's a uniform consistency, remove from the heat, add the pecans, and toss to coat thoroughly.

3. Transfer the pecans to a parchment-lined baking sheet and spread out to create a single layer. Bake for 20 to 25 minutes.

4. Let cool before serving. The sugar and spice coating will harden up a bit and give it a nice crunch. Store them in an airtight container. At room temperature, they should keep for 2 to 3 weeks and in the freezer for much longer.

Ras El Hanout is a gorgeous, North African spice blend. You can use my personal blend in Chapter 1 or find the spice blend at an ethnic grocer. If you are using another blend besides mine, please pay attention to the salt and adjust up or down accordingly in this recipe.

Deviled Eggs Three Ways:
Indonesian, Greek, and Mexican

Deviled eggs was one of my husband's favorite dishes as a kid, a simple food he could make when he came home from school. Since childhood dishes hold the strongest memories, I've come up with numerous different ways to glam up these guys. Here are a few of my favorites. Feel free to experiment and incorporate your own childhood flavors.

INDONESIAN–VEGETARIAN; GREEK–GLUTEN-FREE; AND MEXICAN–VEGETARIAN,
GLUTEN-FREE

YIELDS 24 DEVILED EGGS (EACH)

12 large eggs

For the Indonesian-inspired:

½ cup mayonnaise

2 teaspoons Sambal Oelek (see Chapter 1)

½ teaspoon mustard

pinch sugar

salt, to taste

fried shallot rings, to garnish

For the Greek-inspired:

½ cup Taramosalata (see sidebar)

2 tablespoons Greek yogurt

3 garlic cloves, minced

1½ tablespoons fresh dill, minced

freshly squeezed lemon juice, to taste

salt, to taste

For the Mexican-inspired:
1 Haas avocado, halved, pitted, and peeled
1 jalapeño, seeded and minced
¼ to ½ small red onion, minced (approximately 3 tablespoons)
1 garlic clove, minced
2 tablespoons cilantro, finely chopped
freshly squeezed lime juice, to taste
salt, to taste

1. In a large saucepan, cover the eggs with cold water by 1". Place over high heat and bring to a boil, uncovered so you can watch it. As soon as the water boils, remove from the heat, cover, and let steep for 12 minutes. Drain the eggs and place them in an ice bath (a bowl with ice and water) to cool for 3 to 5 minutes.

2. Carefully, peel the eggs and halve them. Remove the yolks to a medium mixing bowl.

3. *For the Indonesian-, Greek-, and Mexican-inspired separately:* Add all the ingredients to a bowl with the yolks and mash together using a fork. Transfer to a pastry bag fitted with a tip or a plastic bag with one of the corners cut out.

4. Pipe back into the egg halves, finishing the mixture. Chill at least an hour in the refrigerator before serving.

> Taramosalata is a traditional Greek spread made from cured and salted fish roe along with bread and olive oil. Think of it like a caviar spread. You can find it at gourmet and Middle Eastern grocers.

Red Lentil Pâté with Toasted Cashews and Indian Spices

When I'm entertaining, I like to serve a vegetarian pâté like this one—it more than makes up for in flavor what it lacks in fat (like a liver pâté). The inspiration for this is daal, a rich, South Asian lentil dish. Sweet red lentils, tons of fragrant spices, along with aromatics like shallots, chili, garlic, and ginger, make this pâté an unusual but welcome change from the traditional. VEGAN

YIELDS APPROXIMATELY 2½ CUPS

1 cup red split lentils, picked through and rinsed

2 cups water

½ teaspoon turmeric

2–3 tablespoons canola oil

½ teaspoon white cumin seeds

1 large shallot, finely chopped

1 jalapeño or thai green chili, finely chopped

½ teaspoon minced ginger

½ teaspoon ground cumin

½ teaspoon ground coriander

pinch cayenne pepper

4–5 garlic cloves, minced

1 tomato, seeded, strained of juice, and chopped

⅓ cup raw cashews, toasted

freshly squeezed lemon juice, to taste

salt, to taste

small handful of cilantro, finely chopped

crusty bread or crackers, for serving

1. In a medium saucepan, bring lentils with water and turmeric up to a rolling boil over medium-high heat and cook for 10 minutes uncovered. Watch that it's not boiling too hard as it can easily boil over. Skim off any scum as it comes to the top during this period and then, cover and cook another 15 to 20 minutes, until lentils are completely soft and can be mashed. Set aside to cool.

2. Heat a medium skillet over medium heat. Add the oil and the cumin seeds. When they start to sputter (after a minute or so), add the shallots, chili, and ginger and sauté for 3 to 4 minutes, until the shallots are translucent. Add the spices and garlic and sauté for another 30 seconds to a minute, until fragrant. Add the tomatoes and cook until the tomatoes break down and can be mashed. Set aside to cool.

3. Transfer the lentils and the shallot mixture to the bowl of a food processor. Add the raw cashews, a squeeze of lemon juice, and season with salt. Process until the mixture is uniform. Adjust seasoning (it can take quite a bit of salt) and lemon juice to taste.

4. Transfer to a container and refrigerate until completely cooled.

5. Serve garnished with some chopped cilantro and with crusty bread or crackers.

Crispy Roasted Chickpeas with Merkén, Garlic, and Thyme

Crispy chickpeas are a great substitute for traditional mixed nuts for a party food. I learned about a beautifully fragrant spice blend called Merkén while travelling in Chile. Merkén is a flavorful, Chilean spice blend of dried chilies, toasted coriander, and salt. It's fantastic as an all-purpose seasoning (see Chapter 1 for my recipe). It adds heat and nuttiness to the crispy chickpeas here. Rather than frying the chickpeas, I roast them to be a bit healthier. VEGAN, GLUTEN-FREE

SERVES 4–6

2 (15-ounce) cans chickpeas

3 tablespoons olive oil

2 teaspoons Merkén (see Chapter 1)

1 teaspoon granulated garlic

1½ teaspoons dried thyme

salt, to taste

1. Preheat the oven to 400°F.

2. Drain chickpeas of excess liquid and rinse thoroughly. The key to achieving crispy chickpeas is getting them completely dry before roasting, so pat them with towels until there's no more moisture.

3. Place dried chickpeas in a medium bowl and add the remaining ingredients. Toss to make sure they are evenly coated with oil and spices and check seasoning.

4. Spread spiced chickpeas in a single layer on a baking sheet, and roast for 40 to 45 minutes. Take them out after 25 minutes or so, shake them around, and rotate them to achieve even cooking.

5. Let cool before serving. They crisp up as they cool off.

Smoky Eggplant Dip with Fingerling Chips

Chips and dips are a party staple, and this is my slightly fancier version. The eggplant dip is based on baba ganoush, a traditional Middle Eastern mezze of smoky eggplant purée mixed with tahini and extra-virgin olive oil. The smokiness comes from roasting over an open flame, and I add a dollop of crème fraîche and a sprinkling of chives to give it that rich, party-worthy dip feel. Thinly sliced fingerlings fry up in no time for a healthy, homemade chip that is perfect for dipping into the cool, creamy eggplant.

VEGETARIAN, GLUTEN-FREE

SERVES 4–6 (YIELDS APPROXIMATELY 2½ CUPS DIP)

For the eggplant dip:
3 whole Italian eggplants
1 clove Roasted Garlic (see Chapter 1) or 1 clove raw garlic, minced
2 tablespoons tahini
1 tablespoon crème fraîche
juice of ½ lemon
salt, to taste
chives, for garnish

For the fingerling chips:
canola or peanut oil for frying
1 pound fingerling potatoes, scrubbed, skin-on
salt, to finish

1. *For the eggplant dip:* Preheat the oven to 400°F.

2. Prick the eggplants all over with a fork and then place on the open flame of a gas burner. You want to char the skin all over the eggplant to impart smokiness. If you don't have a gas burner, you can do this on a grill or under the broiler.

3. Once the skin is charred and shriveling, transfer to a baking sheet and finish cooking in the oven for another 25 to 30 minutes.

4. Let the eggplants cool before handling. Split them open and scrape out all the flesh inside into a medium bowl. Add the garlic, tahini, crème fraîche, lemon juice, and salt and use a fork to mash everything together. You want to create a creamy consistency but with texture. You can also do this in the food processor if you want something smoother. Taste and readjust seasoning. Chill and garnish with chives before serving.

5. *For the fingerling chips:* In a Dutch oven or large saucepan, heat 2" to 3" of oil to 360°F. The oil should go less than halfway up the pot.

6. Using a mandoline or with a very sharp knife, thinly slice the fingerling potatoes and transfer to a bowl of water. Gently mix the potato slices, strain out the water, and dry on paper towels. The potatoes should be completely dry before adding to the oil or they will spatter and bubble up.

7. Add the fingerling slices to the oil, working in batches. Fry for about 45 seconds to 2 minutes, depending on how thickly you sliced them, until golden brown. Transfer them to a paper towel–lined plate and finish them with salt.

8. Serve the dip cold with fingerling chips on the side.

Homemade Popcorn with Spiced Honey and Butter

Taking the extra step to make homemade popcorn makes a world of difference in the flavor and really doesn't take much more time than the usual method of popping a bag in the microwave. I love relying on all-natural ingredients and playing around with different combos: truffle butter and Parmesan, garlic and black pepper, or even the Japanese spice blend furikake and rice crackers. This version yields kettle corn–like, sweet and savory, fluffy kernels with a hint of spice. If you haven't made my spice-infused honey, you can sub in regular old honey and still get delicious results. VEGETARIAN, GLUTEN-FREE

SERVES 4

¼ cup canola oil

½ cup popcorn kernels

½ stick unsalted butter

1 tablespoon Spiced Honey (see Chapter 1)

¾ teaspoon salt

1. In a medium pot or large saucepan with a cover, add the oil so that it coats the bottom of the pan. Add the popcorn, cover, and place over medium-high heat. When the kernels start to pop, shake the pan until the popping slows to a few seconds between each pop. Shaking the pan will help to prevent the popcorn from burning. Remove from heat.

2. In a small saucepan, melt the butter with the honey and salt. Pour the butter-honey mixture all over the popcorn, tossing to coat.

3. Transfer to a large bowl and serve warm.

Chapter 3

SOUPS AND SALADS

There is something extraordinarily comforting about a silky bowl of soup. The soups in this section work beautifully to complement a main meal and are great in the colder months to warm you up. For me, some of these soup recipes are even substantive enough to have as the main meal itself. The hearty Harira and the Lemon-Egg Soup with Quinoa in particular are filling and have tons of protein.

I like salads to have texture, acid, and brightness to catch my attention. I particularly love the combination of sweet and salty, and you'll see that in almost every salad, I have elements of both. For weeknights, I sometimes like to pair a simply cooked, salt-and-pepper protein with a bright and crunchy salad, so most of these dishes hold their own and work well with a great piece of fish or chicken. I'm also a big believer in letting vegetables and their flavors shine through. Dressings can enhance those flavors but are not meant to dominate a dish. A good seasonal vegetable doesn't need much embellishment at all!

Sopa de Flor de Calabaza (Squash Blossom Soup)

Squash blossoms are the delicate, edible flowers of the zucchini plant and can often be found in summer at the farmers' market. The traditional, Mexican version of this soup purées the squash blossoms right in, but I think they are more beautiful left whole, to finish the soup. With the corn, potatoes, and squash, this soup is silky and rich without any cream, but a dollop of crème fraîche at the end really brings the flavor together. GLUTEN-FREE

SERVES 4–6

2–3 tablespoons unsalted butter

1 large yellow onion, finely chopped

1 jalapeño, finely chopped

2 Yukon gold potatoes, peeled and cut into a small dice

1 medium butternut squash, cut into a small dice

2 garlic cloves, minced

4 cups chicken stock

small bunch of thyme

1 fresh or dried bay leaf

tiny pinch saffron (optional)

3 ears of corn, kernels removed and scraped for juice

salt and freshly ground black pepper, to taste

8–10 large squash blossoms

crème fraîche, for garnish

1. In a soup pot, heat the unsalted butter over medium-low heat. Add the onions and jalapeño and sauté for 4 to 6 minutes, until the onions are translucent. Add the potatoes, squash, and garlic and cook for another 2 minutes.

2. Add in the stock, thyme, bay leaf, and saffron and bring up to a boil. Reduce to a simmer and simmer partially covered for 10 minutes.

3. Now, add in the corn kernels and any juice from the corn and simmer partially covered for another 10 to 15 minutes, until all the vegetables are tender.

4. Remove the thyme bunch and the bay leaf, and purée the soup in a blender, working in batches. Season to taste with salt and freshly ground black pepper.

5. I like the squash blossoms to be slightly raw, so I put two of them in each bowl along with a dollop of crème fraîche and pour the hot soup right over. The soup wilts them just enough. Serve immediately.

Harira

Harira is a gorgeous chickpea, lentil, and tomato soup that hails from Morocco and other parts of North Africa. Each family has its own version, tweaked to their tastes, and here is mine. It's hearty without being too heavy, fragrant from the cinnamon, ginger, and saffron, with a bright lemony finish. I often throw in some chicken and make this my weeknight meal, and it tastes even better the next day. GLUTEN-FREE

SERVES 6–8

2–3 tablespoons olive oil

2 medium yellow onions, finely chopped

½ teaspoon tomato paste

1 cup dried chickpeas, soaked overnight and drained

1 cup Puy lentils, rinsed and picked through

6 cups chicken stock

1 cup canned crushed tomatoes

½ teaspoon turmeric

¼ teaspoon ground ginger

¼ teaspoon ground cinnamon

½ teaspoon hot Hungarian paprika

large pinch saffron

1 fresh or dried bay leaf

½ cup orzo

salt and freshly ground black pepper, to taste

small handful of cilantro and parsley, roughly chopped, for garnish

freshly squeezed lemon juice, to taste

lemon wedges, to garnish

1. Heat a soup pot or Dutch oven over medium heat. Add oil and chopped onions with a bit of salt to draw out the moisture. Sauté until onions are translucent. Add the tomato paste and sauté for another minute or two.

2. Add chickpeas, lentils, stock, crushed tomatoes, spices, and bay leaf. Bring up to a boil and lower to a simmer. Simmer covered for 1 hour.

3. Add orzo and simmer covered for another 20 to 25 minutes, until the pasta is cooked through. Adjust the seasoning at this point and remove the bay leaf.

4. Finish with chopped herbs and lemon juice, to taste. Serve hot, garnished with lemon wedges.

Forgot to soak the dried chickpeas overnight? You can easily substitute canned chickpeas that have been drained and rinsed. Just remember to shorten the cook time, checking after a half hour or so, to accommodate for the change.

Trinidadian-Chinese Wonton Soup

If you're wondering about my last name, LeeKong, this soup is a great way to explain it! My husband's family is from Trinidad, and, like many islands, there are influences from all over. In particular, there's a significant Chinese population, individuals who are descended from the first Chinese immigrants that came over as indentured servants in the early 1800s. Chinese food has become integrated into the culture over the last 200 years, and wontons, fried or in soup, are eaten all over the country. This soup is my version of one that I eat from a little, takeout Trinidadian-Chinese spot in Crown Heights, Brooklyn.

SERVES 8–10

For the wontons:

2 tablespoons canola oil

1 large shallot, finely chopped

½ Scotch bonnet or habanero pepper, seeded and minced

½ teaspoon minced ginger

1 green onion, minced

2–3 garlic cloves, minced

½ pound ground pork, room temperature

zest of 1 lime

¾ teaspoon soy sauce

½ teaspoon Worcestershire sauce

2 tablespoons chopped fresh cilantro

salt and freshly ground black pepper, to taste

36–38 frozen wonton skins, thawed

For the soup:
10 cups chicken stock
¾ teaspoon salt
¼ teaspoon ground white pepper
1½ teaspoons finely chopped chives
sesame oil, to drizzle

1. Heat a small sauté pan over medium heat. Add the oil and, when it's hot, add the shallots, pepper, ginger, and green onion. Sauté for 3 to 4 minutes, until shallots are translucent. Add the garlic and sauté for another 30 seconds to a minute. Set aside to cool.

2. To a large bowl, add the ground pork, lime zest, soy sauce, Worcestershire sauce, and cilantro. Add the cooled shallot mixture and season with salt and freshly ground black pepper. Mix carefully so that the pork stuffing is uniform.

3. Now, make the wontons. Fill a small bowl with water, keeping it to the side, and cover the wonton skins you aren't using and the prepared wontons with a damp paper towel to prevent them from drying out. On a cutting board, lay each wonton skin flat. Add 1 teaspoon of the pork mixture to the center of the wonton skin and, using your finger dipped in the water, brush each edge of the wonton skin with a little water. Fold one corner across to the opposite corner to form a triangle. Then, bring the long corners across to the opposite edge; the result is a pentagon shape. Press firmly along the edges so none of the pork mixture seeps out during cooking—the water should help seal them.

4. In a large stockpot, bring the chicken stock to a boil over high heat and season with salt and pepper. Gently, add the wontons and cook for 5 minutes.

5. Garnish with chopped chives and sesame oil before serving.

Spiced Chestnut Soup

This is one of my favorite soups of all time. The inspiration for it came from an Anglo-Indian soup called mulligatawny, which my Mom made for me growing up. In lieu of using the traditional lentils for the soup, I love to play around with different seasonal ingredients, and this version uses some lovely, sweet chestnuts. This soup is warm and comforting with a beautiful creamy finish . . . enjoy! GLUTEN-FREE

SERVES 4–6 (YIELDS APPROXIMATELY 5½ CUPS)

3 tablespoons unsalted butter

2 shallots, finely chopped

½ teaspoon minced ginger

1 small red chili, finely chopped

¾ teaspoon ground cumin

1 teaspoon ground coriander

½ teaspoon turmeric

⅛ teaspoon cayenne pepper

4–5 garlic cloves, minced

1 pound peeled, cooked whole chestnuts

1 bay leaf

3 cups chicken or vegetable stock

1 (13½-ounce) can coconut milk

3 tablespoons heavy cream

freshly squeezed lemon juice, to taste (can take a few squeezes)

salt, to taste

small handful of cilantro, finely chopped, for garnish

hazelnut or other nut oil, for garnish

1. Heat a Dutch oven or other heavy-bottomed pot over medium-low heat and add butter. Watch closely. When foam subsides, add shallot and a bit of salt to draw out the moisture. Let sweat for a minute or so. Add ginger, chili, cumin, coriander, turmeric, and cayenne. Cook for 5 to 7 minutes, until shallots are translucent and super soft. Add garlic and cook for 30 seconds to 1 minute, until fragrant.

2. Add chestnuts and stir to combine. Let cook for about 2 minutes and then add the bay leaf and stock. Bring up to a boil, lower to a simmer, and simmer covered for 20 to 25 minutes. You want the chestnuts to easily break apart with your wooden spoon.

3. Remove bay leaf and, in a blender or using a hand blender, purée until smooth. Strain if desired to remove any bits. Add coconut milk, heavy cream, and lemon juice, and adjust seasoning to taste.

4. Serve hot with a little fresh chopped cilantro and a drizzle of hazelnut oil on top.

Lemon-Egg Soup with Quinoa

When I was in Peru, I learned all about quinoa: where it's grown in the mountains and how it's eaten throughout the country. One of the best dishes I sampled there was a simple but tasty soup that had chopped vegetables and was thickened with eggs and evaporated milk. My mind immediately imagined using quinoa in avgolemono, a creamy lemon-egg-orzo soup that's served in Greece but also throughout the Mediterranean and Middle East. This recipe became my perfect marriage of the two and is one of my go-to weeknight meals. Here, I use quinoa instead of orzo for a bit of protein, add a few more aromatics, but keep that signature, silky texture and bright lemony flavor. GLUTEN-FREE

SERVES 4–6

1 small red onion, quartered

1 jalapeño, halved, ribs and seeds removed

2–3 garlic cloves

2–3 tablespoons olive oil

1 cup raw quinoa

2 quarts chicken or vegetable stock

1 bay leaf

1 (2") piece of lemon peel

4 eggs, separated

½ cup freshly squeezed lemon juice

salt and freshly ground black pepper, to taste

small handful of parsley, chives, or cilantro, finely chopped, for garnish

1. To the bowl of a food processor, add the red onion, jalapeño, and garlic cloves. Process until finely chopped.

2. Heat a medium pot over medium heat. Add olive oil and the chopped vegetables with a little salt to draw out the moisture. Sweat these out for 4 to 5 minutes, until the red onion is translucent.

3. Add the quinoa to the pot and toast for a minute or two, stirring frequently. Add the stock, bay leaf, and lemon peel and bring up to a boil. Lower to a simmer and simmer covered for 20 minutes, until the quinoa is fully cooked. Remove from the heat.

4. In a small bowl, whisk the egg whites until they have tripled in volume and are foamy. Add the egg yolks and lemon juice to the beaten whites and whisk gently to combine. Ladle some of the hot (not boiling) soup into the egg mixture, whisking at the same time. You want to bring the eggs up to temperature without scrambling, so continue to add ladlefuls of soup until the temperature of the egg mixture is the same as the soup. Add the egg mixture back into the soup and stir for a minute or two to incorporate and create an even, creamy texture. Taste and adjust seasoning.

5. Serve immediately, sprinkled with the fresh herbs. I think cilantro is the most complementary herb here, but go with what you love best.

This soup is a fast one and can be made in less than 25 minutes. If you so happen to have cooked quinoa on hand, this will take you less than 10 minutes and still be bright and flavorful. This soup actually tastes best the same day, but if you are making it ahead of time, it's best to add the eggs and lemon at the last minute for optimal flavor and texture. You *can* still reheat the soup—you just want to do it slowly (on low heat) to prevent the eggs from curdling.

The Art of the Easy Homemade

When I think homemade, I immediately conjure this image of an older woman slaving away in the kitchen for hours. In fact, on many of my trips and in kitchens in New York City, I have met "her"—making breads or Turkish *yufka* dough from scratch; teaching me how to preserve fresh orange, mandarin, and bergamot; or toasting and grinding spices to blended perfection. Like many of us, I love true homemade processes but don't always have the time. I've included my favorite, no-fail pie crust recipe in this book, and, for the holidays and dinner parties, I use it. But on a regular afternoon, if I have a glut of, say, fall apples or summer berries lying around, I may just whip out a little frozen puff pastry and call it a day.

The reality is that homemade doesn't *always* have to translate into long hours and painstaking processes. There are techniques I've learned over the years that are shockingly simple and so, in knowing that they take less than ten minutes to do (less than the time it would take you to go to the grocery store), they become transformative.

It may surprise you, but one of the easiest places to start is with dairy. Heavy cream and a bit of buttermilk that sit together in a bowl on the counter become rich and luscious crème fraîche. Heavy cream in a stand mixer can be whipped into some of the best butter you've tasted. Bring whole milk to a boil, lower to 110°F, add a few tablespoons of "starter yogurt," and after an overnight stay in a warm spot, you get gorgeous, sweet, creamy homemade yogurt that tastes better than anything in the stores. Strain it and you have your own thick, Greek yogurt!

One of the most fun dairy tricks I've learned was taught to me in the Indian kitchens in which I've worked. Making your own fresh cheese takes less than fifteen minutes, ten of which is just bringing the milk and cream up to a boil. Here's how to do it:

- Start with a ½ gallon of milk and 1 cup heavy cream in a medium pot.
- Bring up to a boil, remove from the heat, and add 6 tablespoons of white vinegar.
- Stir once. Stirring too much will toughen up the curds and make them rubbery.

- Let sit 5 minutes; then use a slotted spoon to transfer the curds to a cheesecloth-lined strainer and season with salt. That's it!

Yes, all it takes to make a cheese is milk, acid, and salt at the end! I use cream to bump up the fat and creaminess here. The acid could be buttermilk, vinegar, or lemon juice, but buttermilk can sometimes make the consistency a bit too soft and has an overtly sour flavor. White vinegar for me gives the perfect texture and is reliable—the acidity of a lemon differs from one to the next, so the measurements can change.

From this point, there are a ton of possibilities. After 5 minutes of straining, you have a cottage cheese texture—fluffy and creamy with soft curds. You can lightly rinse them to remove some of the acidic flavor . . . or not. Leave it for more time, 20 minutes or so, to achieve more of a grainy, ricotta texture, and overnight to get an even drier consistency, more like a crumbled queso fresco. Add spices like garlic, cracked pepper, coriander, or even chili flakes during the straining process and infuse even more flavor into your cheese.

After the initial straining, if you press it in the cheesecloth between two baking sheets with weighted cans on top, you'll achieve a texture more like Indian paneer cheese or haloumi after a few hours. This has a really high melting point, so you can slice and grill or even sear it.

Try this bit of "homemade" for any of the salad recipes in this section that call for a little fresh cheese . . . and impress yourself with how easy it is!

Massaged Kale Salad with Pear, Fresh Cheese, and Pomegranate Vinaigrette

Like a lot of people, I try to incorporate healthy, dark, leafy greens into my diet. I'm big on juicing (to counteract my pizza binges . . .) and trying to get the nutrients in their raw form whenever possible. Kale isn't the easiest green to eat raw—it's a bit bitter with a rough texture. What I love about this recipe is the massage technique to soften the leaves—a little salt, lemon juice, and olive oil breaks down the fibers in the leaves and wilts them down just a little bit, making them perfect for eating in salad form. VEGETARIAN, GLUTEN-FREE

SERVES 4

For the salad:

1 bunch (approximately 5 ounces) kale, stemmed, center rib removed, and roughly torn (Tuscan, Russian Red, and Lacinato kales work well)

1½ teaspoons freshly squeezed lemon juice

2 tablespoons extra-virgin olive oil

¼ teaspoon salt

1 Bartlett pear, cut into a medium dice

½ cup crumbled fresh or goat cheese

freshly ground black pepper, to taste

pomegranate arils, for garnish

For the pomegranate vinaigrette:
1 tablespoon storebought or Homemade Pomegranate Molasses
(see Chapter 1)
1¼ teaspoons red wine vinegar
¾ teaspoon honey
pinch cayenne
salt and freshly ground black pepper, to taste
1–2 tablespoons blended canola/olive oil

1. *For the salad*: To a large bowl, add kale, lemon juice, olive oil, and salt and massage together with your fingertips until kale is lightly wilted. Add chopped pear and crumbled cheese.

2. *For the pomegranate vinaigrette*: Whisk together all ingredients except for the oil. Slowly whisk in oil to emulsify.

3. Dress salad lightly with the pomegranate vinaigrette. Finish it with some freshly ground black pepper and garnish with pomegranate arils.

Israeli Couscous Salad with Lemon, Fennel, and Basil

Couscous is one of those blank-slate ingredients that absorbs flavors incredibly well, and here, I love to use it in a salad with lemon and raw, shaved fennel. The combination, along with some torn basil, is fresh and light, great alongside a simple piece of fish or grilled chicken. I personally prefer the texture of Israeli couscous to the traditional kind, but you could really use either. A few ratios to pay attention to here: Israeli couscous requires 1½ cups of liquid for every cup of the raw couscous. In turn, 1 cup of raw Israeli couscous triples to about 3 cups cooked. VEGAN

SERVES 6–8

3 cups vegetable stock or water

2 cups raw Israeli couscous

2–3 tablespoons extra-virgin olive oil, divided

1 fennel bulb, shaved thin, fronds reserved

1 shallot, minced

1 tablespoon lemon zest

juice of ½ to 1 lemon

1 tablespoon sherry vinegar

small handful of basil, hand-torn

salt and freshly ground black pepper, to taste

1. To cook the couscous, bring the vegetable stock or water up to a boil over high heat. Season with salt, add the couscous, cover, and bring back up to a boil. When it comes up to a strong boil, remove from the heat and let sit covered 8 to 10 minutes, until the couscous has absorbed all of the water. Drizzle with extra-virgin olive oil and fluff with a fork. Cool completely.

2. To the cooled couscous, add the shaved fennel along with 2 tablespoons of chopped fennel fronds, the minced shallot, lemon zest, lemon juice, sherry vinegar, and torn basil. Drizzle a bit of extra-virgin olive oil on top and season with salt and freshly ground black pepper. Mix, taste, and adjust seasoning, including the lemon juice.

3. Chill before serving.

Cucumber and Avocado Salad with Yuzu-Honey Dressing

When one of my favorite neighborhood sushi spots closed, I was really disappointed at not being able to eat my beloved cucumber and avocado salad, so I tried to recreate it at home. Here it is, and it's now a staple salad for me during avocado season. The creamy avocados and crisp, watery cucumbers pair beautifully with the sweet, yuzu-spiked dressing and the nutty crunch from the sesame seeds. Enjoy! VEGETARIAN

SERVES 4

3–4 Persian cucumbers, chopped
2 ripe Haas avocados, halved, pitted, peeled, and chopped
½ teaspoon black sesame seeds, toasted
½ teaspoon white sesame seeds, toasted
small handful of cilantro, finely chopped

For the dressing:
2½ teaspoons soy sauce
2 tablespoons rice vinegar
2 teaspoons yuzu juice (see sidebar)
1 teaspoon honey
2 tablespoons sesame oil
salt, to taste

1. In a bowl, toss together the cucumbers and avocados with the sesame seeds and cilantro.

2. For the dressing, whisk together the soy sauce with the rice vinegar, yuzu juice, and honey. Slowly drizzle in the sesame oil, whisking continuously. Taste and adjust seasoning if necessary.

3. Toss salad with dressing, adjust seasoning, and serve immediately.

You can easily find yuzu at any Asian market, but if you don't have any on hand, you can use the citrus of your choice for this dressing.

Peruvian Rhythms

The outdoor markets of Peru were unlike anything I'd ever experienced before. In other places I've been, the produce looks generally similar to other fruits and vegetables I've seen—maybe I'll see one or two items that are new. But in Lima, on my first day there, I was blown away.

Everything was new and unfamiliar, and I started eating right there in the market. I was taken by *tumbo*, which is similar to passionfruit though a bit more tart and floral; *pepino*, a melon that tastes a bit like cucumber; and (my favorite) *lucuma*, a slightly dry fruit with a banana-butterscotch flavor. *Pacay* was like homespun cotton candy all in a tamarind-esque green pod, and *cherimoya* could have been a cousin of the custard apple. Tiny plums from the mango family, tree tomatoes, and herbs like *huacatay* and *paico*—it was straight sensory overload.

The different ajis, or chilies—*limo*, *rocoto*, *amarillo*, *panca*—were all equally tasty and used in different ways in the cuisine. Aji limo is typically eaten raw and in ceviches, whereas aji amarillo is used both raw and cooked and often found in paste form. Rocoto chilies are traditionally chopped for a picante sauce (and unfortunately made my face itch!), and aji panca, the smokier relative, is usually found in its dried state. And that's what's fascinating: not only seeing the different produce or ingredients but understanding how they fit into the culinary vernacular of the cuisine.

We checked out the fish section—large scallops still with their "foot" (as I like to call it) attached; *camarones*, which are actually closer to a freshwater crayfish; and *langostinos*, the salt-water shrimp. The firm-fleshed flounder, grouper, and sole are typically used for ceviche, which is traditionally eaten only at lunchtime to ensure freshness. Lunch is the big meal in Peru, and with the abundance of fresh vegetables, salads like *solterito* (the next recipe) are popular. Lentils are often served to bring wealth.

I went on to learn more about *anticuchos* and the now popular *pollo a la brasa*, along with traditional Creole and Andean cooking. I visited the Urubamba valley and felt how different the cultures of the mountains and country are. I feel like I only scratched the surface while in Peru, and I'm not sure how many visits it will take to gain a better understanding. I haven't even touched on the Amazon, and the biodiversity there alone could warrant months.

Understanding the flows or rhythms of the culture really invites you in, helps you grasp the lifestyle, and gives a clearer picture of the day-to-day existence of people in that part of the world. The next time you take a trip, look beyond restaurants to markets and chat with locals to find out more about their culture, food and otherwise!

Peruvian Fava Bean and Corn Salad (Solterito)

Solterito, meaning "little single man" in Spanish, is a dish that originates in Arequipa, Peru. It's a simple salad that uses local, cheap ingredients—fava or broad beans, Peruvian choclo corn, spicy rocoto chilies, tomato, red onion, olives, and fresh cheese. It's fresh and easy to make, and I love to eat this as the weather turns warmer. Buttery, nutty favas have a relatively short season, so feel free to substitute in edamame or chickpeas to enjoy this dish all the way through the end of summer. VEGETARIAN, GLUTEN-FREE

SERVES 4–6

1 cup fava beans

2 cups cooked corn kernels

½ cup grape tomatoes, halved

½ medium red onion, finely chopped

1 Fresno chili, minced

⅓ cup pitted black olives

juice of 1 lime

salt and freshly ground black pepper, to taste

2–3 tablespoons extra-virgin olive oil

4–6 medium butter lettuce leaves

½ cup queso fresco, crumbled

2 tablespoons chives, finely chopped

1. To cook fava beans, you have to peel them first—twice, actually! (When it comes to fava beans, pick smaller, bright-green pods. The larger, bulging ones are a bit older and may be bitter.) Take the beans out of the pod, then peel away the tough outer layer of each individual bean. Bring water up to a boil in a medium pot, salt heavily, and add peeled beans. Cook for two minutes and then transfer to an ice bath (a bowl with ice and water) to cool completely.

2. In a medium bowl, mix together the fava beans, corn, grape tomatoes, red onion, chili, and black olives. Squeeze the lime juice all over, season with fresh salt and pepper, and drizzle with a few tablespoons of the extra-virgin olive oil. Combine thoroughly, taste, and adjust seasoning.

3. Serve salad chilled on individual butter lettuce leaves. Top with queso fresco and some chopped chives.

Green Mango and Carrot Slaw with Fresh Chili, Peanuts, and Mint

Green mango is found in salads throughout Asia. Green mango is tart, a little sweet, and has that signature musky floral quality. It's beautiful on its own, but I think the sweetness from the carrots in this salad balances out the flavors and adds a lovely crispness. A touch of heat from the chili, some crunch from the toasted peanuts, and brightness from the mint—the salad is simple and addictive. That green chili is strictly for flavor and a touch of heat. Remove it before serving unless you want your diners hopping around the table.

VEGAN, GLUTEN-FREE

SERVES 4–6

2 green mangoes, peeled, pitted, and julienned

2–3 large carrots, peeled and julienned

1–2 Thai green chilies, slit

juice of 1 lime

¾ teaspoon sugar

½ teaspoon salt

small handful of mint, chiffonade

½ cup toasted peanuts, crushed

1. In a large bowl, mix together the julienned green mangoes and carrots; then add the chilies, lime juice, sugar, salt, and mint. Taste, adjust seasoning, and chill in the fridge for at least a half hour before serving. The flavors will marry together as it chills.

2. Serve the salad topped with the crushed peanuts.

Butter Lettuce Salad with Radish, Avocado, and Creamy Sesame-Buttermilk Dressing

Butter lettuce is one of my favorite bases for salads. The leaves look beautiful; have a gorgeous, watery sweetness; and tear easily. For creamy dressings, I often look for alternatives to fatty mayo, and buttermilk provides the perfect texture. It's also a great, tart balance to the nuttiness of tahini here. This is an easy weeknight salad I have fairly often in my house. VEGETARIAN

SERVES 4–6

For the salad:

2 heads of Butter lettuce, separated into leaves

1–2 Haas avocados, peeled, pitted and cut into a medium dice

3–4 radishes, sliced thin

2 teaspoons sesame seeds, lightly toasted

salt and freshly ground black pepper

For the dressing:

2 tablespoons tahini

4 teaspoons soy sauce

3½ teaspoons rice vinegar

¼ cup buttermilk

4 teaspoons sesame oil

4 teaspoons honey

1. For the salad: In a large bowl, toss together the lettuce with the avocados, radishes, and sesame seeds. Season with salt and freshly ground black pepper.

2. For the dressing: In a small bowl, whisk together all the ingredients until uniform.

3. Drizzle salad with dressing before serving.

Chapter 4

FISH AND SEAFOOD

Fish and seafood traditions from around the world are incredibly exciting. This chapter's global influences come from places like Japan to North Africa to, where I went to college, Rhode Island, USA! Texture plays a strong role in this section because I love a little bite and heft to my fish and seafood. Check out my Salt-Baked Fish with Chermoula for instructions on salt-baking, which is one of my favorite (not to mention one of the easiest) methods of cooking fish.

Many of these recipes can be scaled down or split amongst more people to provide a delicious appetizer portion—I left the option up to you, but you can be sure all of these dishes are impressive visually and entertainment-worthy!

Sautéed Rhode Island Calamari with Garlic, Cherry Peppers, and Bread Crumbs

I went to college in Rhode Island and an almost weekly indulgence at a local Italian eatery was a variation of this calamari (explaining the freshman 20++!). The calamari were battered, deep-fried, and tossed with garlic and cherry peppers. After I left the area, to my utter dismay, I couldn't find the dish anywhere, and so I worked on creating my own version. Rather than deep-frying, I give the calamari a quick sauté with a light cornstarch coating and then toss it with the bread crumbs after. It feels healthier this way and gives the calamari an amazing texture. Garlicky, buttery, with heat and acidity from the cherry peppers, it's a lovely food memory that takes me back.

SERVES 4 AS AN APPETIZER (2–3 AS AN ENTRÉE)

1 pound squid, cleaned, tubes cut into ½" rings and tentacles halved

½ cup cornstarch

¾ teaspoon granulated garlic

¾ teaspoon granulated onion

1 teaspoon salt, plus more to taste

½ teaspoon freshly ground black pepper

2–3 tablespoons olive oil

2 tablespoons unsalted butter

4–5 garlic cloves, minced

¼ cup plain bread crumbs

1 cup sliced, pickled cherry peppers (see sidebar)

¼ teaspoon lemon zest

freshly squeezed lemon juice, to taste

small handful of parsley, finely chopped

1. Rinse the squid and pat dry thoroughly using paper towels. In a large bowl, whisk together the cornstarch, granulated garlic, granulated onion, salt, and freshly ground black pepper. Dredge the squid in the cornstarch mixture, shaking off as much of the excess as possible. You want a very light coating here.

2. Heat a large sauté pan over high heat. When it's hot, add the olive oil to coat the bottom of the pan and then add the squid. Let them sit for one minute in the hot pan and then toss them around, sautéing for the next minute to 90 seconds to develop a little golden color. Remove with a slotted spoon to a paper towel–lined plate. If the squid don't fit in your pan in a single, spaced-out layer, work in batches here and repeat the process.

3. Reduce the heat to medium-low and add the butter. When it has melted, throw in the garlic and the bread crumbs and toast for a minute or so, until the bread crumbs deepen in color and the garlic turns fragrant. Add the cherry peppers, heat through for about 30 seconds, and then add the squid back in, tossing to coat completely with the bread crumbs and the garlic.

4. Finish by adding to the pan the lemon zest, lemon juice, parsley, and a bit of salt to taste. Serve immediately.

Can't find cherry peppers? Or are they too hot for your taste? You can use mild banana pepper rings or even sliced pickled jalapeños instead. (Both are jarred and found in the pickled or ethnic section of the grocery.) I've tried both in a pinch when I didn't have the cherry peppers on hand, and they work beautifully.

Wandering Brazil

Many (many!) years ago, I took a trip to Brazil with a girlfriend. It was ridiculously carefree, and we wandered the streets of Salvador, Bahia, trolling for local jewelry, listening to the local Afro-Brazilian band Olodum, and eating Brazilian food in our bikinis. I picked up an amazing painting I found down a side street for my (then) boyfriend and spent the days debating which beach was the most beautiful.

Ten years later, I took a trip back with my (now) husband. We did a bit of wandering ourselves (though eating in a bikini at this age was *out* of the question), and we had the fortune of stumbling on the same painter. It felt like destiny! I got him another piece to go with the first one, and both now hang in our apartment.

Instead of hanging at the beach, this time I checked out a few kitchens and spent days in local markets to get a sense of the food, fascinated by the multiethnic cuisine of the country. The historical influences are staggering, with the native indigenous, the colonizing Portuguese, and the African slave populations providing the most heavy-handed impact. Other Europeans (including German, Italian, and Spanish), the Japanese, and the Lebanese immigrated to the country, and their food is represented as well.

Feijoada (see Chapter 6) is the national dish of Brazil and truly one of my favorites. But during that trip with my girlfriend, I tasted *moqueca* for the first time, and it instantly stole my heart. We were on a tiny street at a restaurant, whose name washed away with the *caipirinhas* I drank, and I even brought home the leftovers that night and attempted to stash them in the hotel minibar for later consumption (difficult, but it worked!).

So all I could think about when I went back was learning how to make this dish, and I was lucky enough to learn it firsthand. There are a number of types of *moqueca* in the country, but what I learned is *moqueca baiana*. This dish reflects the African influence in the region, being a seafood stew with onions, peppers, *dende* (palm oil), and coconut milk. Of course, I've modified the tradition for my own use, and it's now the base for my favorite mussel dish (Mussels with African Chilies and Coconut)—rich, with heat from the chilies and that creaminess from the coconut.

There are so many places in Brazil I have yet to visit, and I cannot wait to continue to explore more in the years to come. And maybe pick up another painting . . . .

Mussels with African Chilies and Coconut (Moqueca-Style)

One of the most famous dishes in Brazil is moqueca, a typical seafood stew with onions, peppers, and coconut milk, and I thought it would be perfect as a base for mussels. Dende oil is the local palm oil they use—it imparts the dish with distinctive flavor and a beautiful orange hue. Feel free to substitute canola or another vegetable oil (a bit healthier any-way), and remember to watch out for those dried chilies when you are eating! They are killer . . . . GLUTEN-FREE

SERVES 4

3–4 tablespoons dende or canola oil

6–8 dried African bird's eye chilies

4 shallots, finely chopped

1 red or yellow bell pepper, finely chopped

8 cloves of garlic, minced

½ cup white wine

1 cup fish or vegetable stock

2 (13½-ounce) cans coconut milk

handful of cilantro, finely chopped

salt, to taste

4 pounds fresh mussels, scrubbed and debearded (see sidebar)

2–3 green onions, green and light green parts only, thinly sliced

squeeze of lime juice

toasted crusty bread, for serving

1. Heat a medium pot or Dutch oven over medium heat. Add oil and chilies and sauté briefly (a minute or two to infuse the oil). Add shallots and bell pepper and a pinch of salt to draw out the moisture. When shallots are translucent (3 to 4 minutes), add minced garlic and cook for 30 seconds or so, until fragrant.

2. Add the white wine and reduce until it's almost completely gone. Add the fish or vegetable stock, the coconut milk, and 1 or 2 tablespoons of the chopped cilantro. Bring up to a boil and lower to a simmer. Simmer uncovered for 5 to 7 minutes, until the liquid has reduced by half. Taste and adjust seasoning at this point.

3. Throw in the mussels and green onions. Bring temperature up to a simmer again, and cook covered for a few minutes, until mussels open. Mine took somewhere between 3 and 4 minutes—you don't want to overcook.

4. Squeeze fresh lime juice over mussels, transfer to a bowl, and sprinkle remaining cilantro on top. Serve hot with big pieces of toasted, crusty bread.

A key to making delicious mussels is thoroughly cleaning them. I like to scrape around the outside of each mussel with a paring knife, removing any debris and hairy parts (beard). Prepare a bowl of cold water and add sea salt until the water tastes pretty salty. Rinse off the scraped mussels, place in the bowl of salt water, and refrigerate for a minimum of a half hour. The mussels will release a lot of their sand and grit this way. Remember to rinse again before cooking and discard any open mussels.

Charred Honey-Miso Smoked Salmon

This is an incredibly easy fish dish with a foolproof, 10-minute smoking method that I love to use. A quick smoke, a dip in a simple marinade, and then on to the pan. Asian flavors work great with an oily fish like this—I use it for Arctic Char as well. The miso and honey give a glazed sweetness that works beautifully. I like to leave the skin on to have that salty, crisp texture against the tender flesh of the salmon, and because of the sugars in the marinade, the skin looks a bit more charred than it tastes. But you can use this smoking method and marinade on a skinless fillet and get great results too!

SERVES 4

a piece of coal

canola oil, to drizzle

4 (6–8-ounce) fillets salmon, skin on

¼ cup sweet white miso

¼ cup mirin

3 tablespoons honey

1 tablespoon ponzu, or 1 squeeze of lemon juice

salt, to taste

2–3 tablespoons canola oil

1. The first step is to smoke the salmon—we're going to use a cold-smoking process. Place a very small (small enough to hold a piece of coal) metal bowl in a much larger metal bowl. Line the little bowl with foil and then place the salmon fillets, flesh-side up, in the larger bowl around the little bowl. Light a piece of coal, place it in the foil-lined little bowl, and drizzle the coal with a little oil. Place plastic wrap over the larger bowl and let smoke for 10 minutes.

2. In a small saucepan, whisk together the miso, mirin, honey, and ponzu over medium-low heat. Let the mixture come up to a simmer and simmer briefly, just until all of the ingredients have incorporated and the mixture is smooth and uniform. Remove from heat and let cool.

3. Place the smoked salmon pieces in a plastic bag and then add in the cooled marinade. Refrigerate for a minimum of a half hour, but it's best to let it sit overnight.

4. Remove the salmon from the marinade, wipe the marinade completely off the fish, and dry the fish thoroughly with paper towels. Season the skin-side with a bit of salt. Heat a large sauté pan over medium-high heat and add the oil. Place the salmon fillets skin-side down in the pan, reduce the heat to medium-low, and hold them down with your fingers or a fish spatula to make sure they're flush with the pan.

5. Usually, I let the fish cook on this side for the full time, but because of the sugars in the marinade, the skin will burn. Flip the fish after 2 to 3 minutes, once the skin is crisped, and let it finish cooking on the flesh side to desired cooking temperature, usually another 3 to 4 minutes for medium-rare. The skin should look a bit charred but will taste salty and crispy, not burnt.

6. Serve immediately.

Chicken Fried Scallops

These are my rendition of the fried scallops I've tasted from Korean markets in Brooklyn. I do them chicken fried–style! They are crispy, succulent, and perfectly cooked each time. Try these with a bit of tartar sauce or even some soy-garlic dipping sauce.

SERVES 4

1 pound large, dry sea scallops (approximately 12 to 16)

½ cup all-purpose flour

¼ cup cornstarch

¾ teaspoon salt, plus more to finish

¾ teaspoon black pepper

1 teaspoon granulated garlic

1 teaspoon granulated onion

¼ teaspoon cayenne pepper

½ cup buttermilk

1 egg

¼ teaspoon Dijon mustard

couple splashes of hot sauce, or ½ teaspoon sriracha

canola or peanut oil, for frying

1. To prepare the scallops, remove the small muscle and then rinse and dry them thoroughly.

2. Set up a dredging station. Mix together the all-purpose flour, cornstarch, salt, black pepper, granulated garlic, granulated onion, and cayenne in one bowl. In another, beat together the buttermilk, egg, Dijon, and hot sauce. Dredge the scallops in the flour mixture, dusting off any excess. Dip in the buttermilk mixture and let the excess drip off once again. Then place back into the flour mixture to get a nice coating. Place on a wire rack while you finish the process for all the scallops.

3. Heat 2" to 3" of oil in a Dutch oven or a deep-fryer to 360°F. Fry scallops in batches for 3 to 4 minutes, until golden and crisp, and drain on paper towels. While hot out of the oil, season with a little bit of salt. Serve immediately with the dipping sauce of your choice.

These take no time to make, but if you want to do some of it ahead of time, you can prep them to the point that they are battered and keep them in the fridge until ready to fry and serve. Fry and serve right away, though, because they do tend to get a bit soggy if they sit for too long.

Creole Shrimp and Grits

There is no way to say no to shrimp and grits. It's an incredible meal, and here I put my time spent in New Orleans to good use. My Creole spice blend is packed with flavor and a touch of heat, and when you cook it up with the shrimp, shallots, and a few pats of butter, the pan drippings are divine. In lieu of adding bacon or sausage here, I used smoked mozzarella to give the creamy grits some of that signature smokiness. This dish has serious body, and I love it for dinner as much as I do for brunch.

SERVES 4–6

2 cups milk

2 cups chicken stock

salt and freshly ground black pepper, to taste

1 cup stone-ground grits

5 tablespoons unsalted butter, divided

1½ cups smoked mozzarella, grated

1 pound shrimp, peeled and deveined

3½ teaspoons NOLA Creole Seasoning (see Chapter 1)

3 tablespoons olive oil

1 shallot, minced

1 jalapeño, seeded, deveined, and minced

chopped green onions and parsley, for garnish

1. In a saucepan, bring milk and chicken stock up to a boil. Lower to a simmer, season with salt and pepper, and whisk in grits. Cover and cook at a low simmer for 25 to 30 minutes. Remove from the heat and add in 3 tablespoons of the butter along with the smoked mozzarella, whisking to incorporate fully. Keep covered and warm.

2. Make sure the shrimp are dry and toss with the NOLA Creole Seasoning and some salt. Heat a skillet over medium-high heat and add the olive oil. Add shrimp in a single layer and cook for a minute and a half. Flip shrimp, lower heat to medium-low, and add in the remaining 2 tablespoons of butter along with the shallots and jalapeño, tossing to combine. Cook for another 2 minutes.

3. Serve grits hot and spoon shrimp mixture on top, letting some of the pan juices drip onto the grits. Garnish with some chopped green onions and parsley.

Over the years, the Creole food of Louisiana has come to represent a blend of all the cultures that inhabit the state—French, Spanish, African, Native American, Portuguese, Caribbean, Irish, Italian, and German.

My Thanksgiving Mashup

Growing up in Florida, Thanksgiving was *the* central holiday in my family and my personal favorite! I was lucky to have a bunch of family who lived in the area, and Thanksgiving was always held at my house. I actually still go down for it each year.

My family does it big, with days of planning and prep and *way* too much food. I still love the coming together of friends and family of all ages; the hustle in the kitchen with my mom and me and whomever else wants to jump in; and the beautiful cool, fall weather (yes, even in Florida). Ours is a whole-day affair, with people stopping by at different points in the meal and card games at the kitchen table later (they get raucous!), followed by a second session of eating in the evening.

Our table is a complete mashup! We start with a lovely, baked Brie served alongside pani puri, which is a *chaat* or a South Asian street snack—these get inhaled as people are arriving and my mom and I are sweating and putting the finishing touches on the main meal. The centerpiece is always a humungous turkey (filled with my mom's stuffing) that my dad carves to perfection. Beef tenderloin, my famous short ribs, or even South African bobotie (see Chapter 6) have been known to pop up on the menu along with daal (South Asian lentils), rice, a massive chopped salad, and everything from a seven-layer dip to corn pudding to African mogo (cassava). Ah, yes, and there is always a vat of sangria on hand, spiked for the adults but with a kid-friendly version too.

Now that I'm married to a guy from Brooklyn with a Trinidadian heritage, this table has been refined further to include dishes he grew up eating—macaroni pie (on the next page), peas and rice—and this year I'm bringing in the stewed oxtail! It does sound all over the place, but when it comes together on the table, it makes perfect sense: the joining of families, traditions, and cultures mirrored in a single meal. It's a completely personalized expression, and mine happens to have South Asian, African, West Indian, and definitively American influences. Even though Thanksgiving is an "American" holiday with traditional foods, I love the idea of leaving the main turkey traditional and experimenting a bit with sides—try tweaking the standard menu to incorporate other aspects of your family's heritage . . . .

Lobster Macaroni Pie with Bacon Bread Crumbs

Macaroni pie is a dish I learned from my husband's side of the family. It's a Trinidadian version of baked mac 'n' cheese with onions, garlic, and Scotch bonnet pepper. I love trying different variations on this, and here's one with beautiful chunks of lobster. Of course, bacon and lobster are meant for each other, so I pulsed some crisp bacon with bread crumbs to make a nice, smoky, crunchy topping. This version is creamy and soul-satisfying with a bit of kick from the chili. The base of this recipe is very versatile, so you can make this into a simple (meaning no lobster/bacon) macaroni pie or throw in your favorite ingredients for your own variation.

SERVES 8–10

2 slices thinly cut bacon, finely chopped

¼ cup bread crumbs

olive oil, as needed

1 large yellow onion, finely chopped

½ Scotch bonnet or habanero pepper, seeded and minced

3 garlic cloves, minced

1 stick unsalted butter

½ cup all-purpose flour

1 quart milk

½ teaspoon ground white pepper

½ teaspoon ground black pepper

a few dashes of hot sauce

2 teaspoons salt

2 eggs, beaten

2½ cups grated Gruyère

1 pound pasta of your choice

¾ pound cooked lobster meat, roughly chopped

1 tablespoon fresh chives, finely chopped

1½ teaspoons fresh thyme, finely chopped

salt, to taste

1. Preheat oven to 350°F.

2. Heat a medium skillet over medium-high heat. Add bacon and cook until brown and crisp. Remove to a paper towel–lined plate using a slotted spoon, leaving the drippings in the pan, and remove the pan from the heat. Let the bacon cool and then transfer the crisp bacon to a food processor with the bread crumbs. Pulse until an even texture is achieved and set aside.

3. Place the pan back over medium heat. You can choose to cook using the bacon drippings (which is what I do) or remove them and add olive oil to the pan. Add in the onion and pepper and cook for 3 to 5 minutes, until the onion is translucent. Add garlic and cook for 30 seconds or so, until fragrant. Remove from heat and cool in a bowl.

4. In a medium saucepan over medium heat, melt butter to start your béchamel. Add flour all at once and whisk vigorously to avoid lumps. Cook for 2 to 3 minutes. You just want to remove the raw taste. Add milk, spices, hot sauce, and salt and continue to whisk to prevent lumps (remember to get the corners!). Once the mixture starts to bubble, reduce heat to low and cook for 5 to 6 minutes, whisking often. Remove from heat.

5. Temper the eggs with the béchamel—ladle a bit of béchamel into the beaten eggs and whisk. Continue adding ladlefuls and whisking until the eggs have been brought up to temperature. Add the eggs into the béchamel and whisk to combine. Add the cheese and whisk until it's melted.

6. Add pasta to boiling, heavily salted water and cook until it's a bit underdone. (The cooking time depends on what type of pasta you are using; check the package.) Drain pasta and add to the béchamel/cheese mixture. Add in the cooled onion mixture along with the lobster meat, chopped chives, and thyme and combine thoroughly. Adjust seasoning at this point and pour into a heavily greased, 3-quart baking dish.

7. Top the macaroni pie with the bacon bread crumbs and bake for 35 minutes, until top is browned and bubbly.

8. Let cool slightly before serving.

Crab Cakes with Mustard Seeds and Parsnips

Crab cakes are a go-to party appetizer for me but also work incredibly well for dinner with a simple salad. After much experimentation, I found parsnips as a binding agent (rather than potatoes) provide the perfect silky texture and complementary sweetness to the crabmeat, and using them also allows you to stretch a bit and get more yield with that expensive crabmeat. Mustard seeds, shallots, chilies, and garlic make these super flavorful, and I prefer pan-frying to deep-frying to keep the calories down. Enjoy!

SERVES 4–6 (YIELDS 15–16 CRAB CAKES)

1 medium parsnip, peeled and cut into a medium dice

2–3 tablespoons canola oil, plus more for frying

1 teaspoon black or brown mustard seeds

8 curry leaves (optional)

1 large shallot, finely minced

1–2 red and/or green chilies, finely chopped (red jalapeño, jalapeño, Thai)

3–4 garlic cloves, minced

1 pound jumbo lump or lump crabmeat, drained and picked through for any shells

¾ cup bread crumbs

1 egg, lightly beaten

½ teaspoon salt

¼ teaspoon freshly ground black pepper

handful of fresh herbs (chives, cilantro, parsley), roughly chopped

1 tablespoon unsalted butter, for frying

salt, to taste

1. In a medium pot, cover parsnips with cold water by about 1". Bring up to a boil and cook for 6 to 8 minutes, until fork-tender. Drain, pass through a ricer (best) or mash with a potato masher, and let cool.

2. While the parsnips are cooking, heat 2 to 3 tablespoons of oil in a medium saucepan over medium-high heat. Add mustard seeds and curry leaves, if using, and when they start to pop after a minute or so, reduce the heat to medium-low and add the shallots, chilies, and garlic. Sauté for 2 to 3 minutes, until the shallots are translucent, remove from heat, and let cool.

3. In a medium bowl, combine crab with the puréed parsnips, the shallot mixture, bread crumbs, egg, salt, pepper, and herbs. Form into 2¼" patties and let chill in the refrigerator for 15 minutes.

4. In a large sauté pan, heat ⅛" of oil with 1 tablespoon of butter. Fry each crab cake 1 to 2 minutes per side, until golden brown, and remove to a paper towel–lined plate to drain.

5. Finish crab cakes with a sprinkle of salt as soon as they are out of the oil and serve hot.

These crab cakes freeze really well, and I love to make a double batch to keep some on hand for a quick weeknight meal. Simply freeze them after you form them into patties. Just let them thaw for a few hours in the fridge before frying them up!

Salt-Baked Fish with Chermoula

Salt-baking is one of my favorite techniques for cooking a whole fish. It's one of those methods where simplicity and minimal labor yield extraordinary results—tender, moist, flaky fish that can be spooned off the bone. Going with the simplicity theme, the sauce chermoula, a North African fish marinade, can be made in five minutes in the food processor and adds a gorgeous tart and spicy angle to the dish. GLUTEN-FREE

SERVES 2–3

For the chermoula:

1 cup cilantro leaves with tender stems

1 cup flat-leaf parsley leaves

3 garlic cloves

1 teaspoon turmeric

1 tablespoon ground cumin

1 teaspoon salt

1 tablespoon sweet paprika

1 teaspoon ground ginger

pinch cayenne

juice of ½ lemon

blended oil, to emulsify

For the fish:

1 whole (2½-pound) black sea bass, snapper, or branzino, cleaned, gutted with top and bottom fins and scales removed

4 cups kosher salt

8 egg whites, beaten

1. Preheat the oven to 400°F.

2. *For the chermoula:* To the bowl of the food processor, add the cilantro, parsley, garlic, spices, and lemon juice. Pulse until chopped. With the food processor on, stream in the oil until everything moves and chops up to be super fine.

3. *For the salt-baked fish:* Place the fish on a work surface and make sure it's dry. Place a tablespoon or so of the chermoula in the inner cavity of the fish.

4. In a bowl, mix together the kosher salt and egg whites with a fork until uniform. Make a bed using ⅓ of the salt mixture on a baking sheet and lay the fish across it. Spoon the remaining salt mixture on top and pat to create a sealed cover across the body of the fish.

5. Place the baking sheet in the oven and roast for 25 to 30 minutes. Let rest a few minutes and then crack open the salt layer with a spoon and peel back the skin. Serve the flesh hot, drizzled with the chermoula.

Paella de Marisco

Paella is one of those irresistible, one-pot meals. This seafood version has layers of shrimp, fish, mussels, and clams, is scented with saffron and smoked Spanish paprika, and forms beautiful soccarat, that crusty layer at the bottom of the paella pan. You can change this up by using some chicken thighs instead of seafood (sear, then let them simmer with the rice, and finish cooking in the oven), or even try different types of seafood: squid and lobster work great in this recipe too. No matter how you make it, this dish is built for entertaining and can feed a crowd. Why not go traditional? Eat straight from the pan!

SERVES 6–8

2–3 tablespoons olive oil

2 links of chorizo, sliced

½ pound large shrimp (approximately 8–10), peeled and deveined

1 pound white flaky fish fillets (like snapper, sea bass, or branzino), skin removed and cut into chunks

1 large yellow onion, chopped

2 small sweet or bell peppers, chopped

8 garlic cloves, minced

1 plum tomato, seeded and chopped

1½ teaspoons fresh thyme leaves, finely chopped

1 teaspoon smoked Spanish paprika

pinch saffron

pinch chili flakes

2½ cups bomba or calasparra rice (paella rice)

6 cups seafood or chicken stock

½ pound mussels (approximately 2 dozen), cleaned

1½ pounds littleneck clams (approximately 1 dozen), cleaned

small handful of parsley, chopped
1 lemon, cut into wedges
salt and freshly ground black pepper, to taste

1. Preheat the oven to 350°F.

2. In a 13" paella pan or a sauté pan with high sides, heat the oil over medium-high heat. Add the sliced chorizo and cook for 3 to 4 minutes to brown. Remove using a slotted spoon to a plate. Dry off and season the shrimp and add them to the pan. Brown for 2 to 3 minutes and then remove to the same plate. Repeat with the fish.

3. Reduce heat to medium-low, add the onions, peppers, and a bit of salt to draw out the moisture. Cook for 4 to 6 minutes, until the onions are translucent. Add the garlic and sauté another 30 seconds to a minute, until fragrant. Add the tomato, thyme, smoked Spanish paprika, saffron, and chili flakes and sauté for another 2 to 3 minutes.

4. Add the rice, season generously with salt, toast for a minute or two, and add the stock. Increase the temperature—you want to bring it up to a boil and then lower to a simmer. Stir just to mix and then leave it. Let simmer uncovered for 15 minutes.

5. Remove from the heat and stir in the chorizo, shrimp, and fish. Layer the mussels and clams on top and place in the oven uncovered for 10 minutes. Remove from the oven and cover with foil, off the heat, for another 10 minutes.

6. Taste and adjust seasoning. Garnish with a little chopped parsley and lemon wedges before serving.

Tiradito with "Leche de Tigre"

I learned this simple preparation while traveling in Peru—tiradito is similar to sashimi, thanks to the influence of Japanese immigrants on Peruvian cuisine. The key here is the leche de tigre, which translates to "tiger's milk" and is the lime juice marinade that cures the fish here. In many spots in Peru, leche de tigre is served in shot glasses as a potion that's supposed to make you strong and act as an aphrodisiac. GLUTEN-FREE

SERVES 4–6 AS AN APPETIZER

½ pound flounder, halibut, or other whitefish

juice of 14 key limes (approximately ⅓ cup)

1 aji limo, jalapeño, or Thai chili, thinly sliced

¼" knob ginger, julienned

½ shallot, minced

1 teaspoon aji amarillo or other chili paste

1–2 teaspoons chopped cilantro, for garnish

salt, to taste

1. Thinly slice the fish and reserve a few scraps for the leche de tigre. Refrigerate the sliced fish.

2. *For the leche de tigre:* To a small bowl, add the fish scraps, lime juice, sliced chili, ginger, and shallot and sprinkle with a bit of salt. Mix together, cover, and refrigerate for 10 to 15 minutes.

3. Arrange the thinly sliced fish on plates. Discard the fish scraps from the leche de tigre and spoon the marinade over the fish slices on the plate so that each is covered. Dot the fish with the chili paste and garnish with the cilantro. Finish with a bit more salt, if desired.

4. Serve immediately.

Chapter 5

POULTRY

When it comes to poultry, flavor is king, and while I have nothing against boneless, skinless chicken breasts and use them for my Turkish-influenced, no-mayo chicken salad, I'm actually inspired by bones and skin. To me, the skin is one of the most important and flavorful parts of a bird, as long as it's cooked right and crackling crisp—you won't find any floppy skin recipes in here! The bones add flavor for stocks and sauces and to the chicken itself as it cooks, and besides, it's always less expensive to opt for cuts with bone!

Veering off the traditional chicken as poultry, I've also included one of my favorite recipes, which I learned while I was in Peru: Arroz Con Pato, or rice with duck, which is a lot more interesting than it sounds. If you've never cooked with it before, here is your chance, and you won't be disappointed! Cornish game hens and turkey drumsticks are also featured here in unusual ways. Many of the recipes in this chapter are meant for weeknight consumption—a faster way to roast a whole chicken, a Spanish-inspired crispy baked chicken with vegetables that does the work for you while in the oven, and a 20-minute stovetop brick chicken. Enjoy!

Butterflied Za'atar Roast Chicken

A good roasted chicken recipe should be part of every cook's arsenal. The key to this truly juicy, crispy chicken is spatchcocking, a butterflying technique that results in perfectly cooked chicken in almost half the time of traditional roasted chicken. Za'atar is a Middle Eastern spice blend that's herbaceous, pairs beautifully with chicken, and creates the signature flavor for this dish. This, to me, is simple enough to create the perfect weeknight meal but also has an elegant touch and is great for easy entertaining.

GLUTEN-FREE

SERVES 4–6

1 (4–5-pound) roasting chicken

2 tablespoons Za'atar (see Chapter 1, or in grocery and specialty stores)

1½ teaspoons granulated garlic

¼ teaspoon lime zest

olive oil, to coat

salt and freshly ground black pepper, to taste

1. Spatchcocking sounds super complicated but isn't. Start with the chicken breast-side down and have some kitchen shears by your side. Starting at the bottom of the bird, cut along each side of the backbone straight through the ribs to the neck opening. Set aside the backbone and giblets and reserve for making stock. Take each side of the flaps in front of you and open the chicken up flat. Flip onto the other side and press down on the breastbone to flatten. Done.

2. There are a few keys to a crispy, succulent roast chicken. First, the chicken must be completely dry. I like to place it, uncovered, on a rack on a baking sheet on a low shelf in the fridge (not touching anything!). I leave it there for a couple of hours or even up to a day. The air circulates and dries out the chicken from all sides. Second, the chicken has to be at room temperature before putting it in the oven. Take it out of the fridge at least an hour before you plan to cook.

3. Preheat the oven to 450°F. Make sure the rack is in the middle of the oven.

4. In a small bowl, mix together the za'atar, garlic, and lime zest. Rub the bird on all sides with olive oil. Sprinkle the za'atar mixture all over and then season *generously* with salt and freshly ground black pepper.

5. Place the chicken skin-side up on a rack on a baking sheet and put into the oven. Face the sheet so the legs go in first—since they take a tad bit longer to cook, this makes sure they are in the hottest part of the oven.

6. Drop the temperature to 400°F and roast for 40 to 50 minutes, until the skin is brown and crispy.

7. The safe internal temperature of cooked chicken is 165°F. I check the temperature with a thermometer inserted into the thigh joint and actually take mine out of the oven around 155°F. I then rest it on a cutting board for 15 minutes tented in foil to finish cooking.

8. Slice (the juices should run clear) and serve!

Arroz Con Pato

A classic dish in Spanish and Latin culture is Arroz con Pollo, or chicken with rice. It's a family-style, one-pot dish—chicken cooked with onions, peppers, garlic, tomatoes, and rice. One of the best dishes I tried in Peru was Arroz con Pato, where succulent duck replaces the chicken in the traditional dish. Two of the differences between Arroz con Pollo and Arroz con Pato (aside from the whole chicken vs. duck thing) is that chicha, Peruvian corn beer, is used to cook the rice and duck in Arroz con Pato. Also, cilantro is blended with water and added to the braising liquid, so the color of the dish takes on a gorgeous, green hue. Beer, cilantro, and duck? A winning combination in my book! I substituted a good stout beer for the traditional corn beer here and a jalapeño in lieu of a Peruvian chili. Also, I went with a shorter grain paella rice because I think the texture is better this way. This dish requires time and a bit of finesse but is well worth it!

SERVES 4–6

approximately 3 pounds duck, preferably 2 legs,
bone-in with thigh meat, and 1 breast, boneless split

salt and freshly ground black pepper, to taste

canola oil

3 shallots, finely chopped

1 jalapeño, minced

2 teaspoons ground cumin

5 garlic cloves, minced

¾ cup stout beer

¼ cup Pisco liqueur (optional)

4 cups chicken stock, divided

1 very large handful cilantro (no tough stems but soft stems are fine), divided

bay leaf, dried or fresh

2½ cups bomba or calasparra rice (paella rice)

¾ cup fresh or frozen peas

1 cup bell pepper, small dice (mixed yellow, red, and orange)

black olives, for garnish

1. Preheat the oven to 350°F.

2. Start by prepping the duck. Dry the legs and breast and trim of excess fat. I like to reserve this fat to melt down and keep for cooking in the future. Prick the legs all over with a fork (this will help the legs render the fat easier) and season all over with salt and freshly ground black pepper. Score the skin on the breast in a crisscross pattern (again for fat-rendering purposes) and refrigerate until a half hour or so before the rice is ready.

3. Heat a large pot or Dutch oven over medium-low heat. Add oil to coat the bottom of the pot and prevent the duck from sticking. Add the legs skin-side down. You want the fat to render out and the skin to crisp and brown. This should take 3 to 4 minutes. Turn pieces over and cook for another 3 minutes. Remove legs to a plate and set aside. Pour off (and keep!) any excess fat, reserving a few tablespoons in the pot for cooking the vegetables.

4. Add shallots, minced jalapeño, and cumin to the pot and cook for 3 to 5 minutes, until the shallots are softened and translucent. Add the minced garlic and cook for another minute. Pour in the beer and

Pisco, if using, and increase the heat. Scrape the bottom of the pan with your spoon to dislodge any brown bits and bring up to a boil.

5. While the vegetables are cooking, blend 2 cups of the chicken stock in a blender with a large handful of the cilantro, reserving a small handful to chop for garnish later. You want to blend on high for several minutes, until the cilantro is totally pulverized.

6. Nestle the duck legs back into the pot, skin-side up. Add the chicken stock blended with the cilantro and a bay leaf, cover, and bring up to a boil. As soon as it boils, place covered pot into the oven and cook for 1½ hours.

7. Take pot out of the oven, place on the stovetop, and temporarily (and carefully) remove the duck legs. Add the rice, peas, and chopped peppers and season very well with salt now to avoid stirring once it's cooked. Add the remaining 2 cups of chicken stock, stir, and nestle the duck thighs back in. Cover and bring back up to a boil. Place in the oven for another 30 to 40 minutes, until the rice is cooked through.

8. In the last 10 minutes of cooking, heat a skillet over medium-low heat. Season scored duck breast all over with salt and freshly ground black pepper. Add a touch of oil to prevent the duck breast from sticking and place breast pieces skin-side down. You want to render all of the fat out, so as the fat accumulates in the pan, carefully pour it off (and keep!). Cook for 8 to 10 minutes until the skin has become crisp and there is no layer of fat underneath it. Turn breast pieces over, increase heat to medium-high, and cook for another 2 minutes. This will yield a medium-rare breast—cook for longer if you like your meat more well done.

9. Remove the duck breast to a cutting board, cover loosely with foil, and let rest for 5 minutes. Thinly slice the duck breast.

10. Serve the rice garnished with black olives, some fresh cilantro, and sliced duck breast.

I view the rendering of fat from duck breast as an art rather than a skill. It requires patience, care, and vigilance. A lot of people think in order to crisp skin, you have to use high heat. Not so. A high heat will actually burn the skin before all of the fat renders out. With a duck breast, you want to score the skin and then use a medium-low heat to slowly coax the fat out from under the skin, pouring off the accumulated fat as you go. It's a rewarding and slightly hypnotic task that is one of the joys of cooking—once you've mastered a crisp duck breast, it will forever be part of your culinary arsenal.

Kenyan Coconut-Coriander Chicken

An aunt on my father's side used to make this dish for me growing up—an East African tradition called kuku paka. Hers involved a lot more fanfare—parboiling the chicken to create stock and then roasting until golden brown while the sauce is simmering—but I wanted to share my simpler way of doing it. The taste is flavorful with heat from the chilies, creaminess from the coconut, and that bright cilantro flavor. GLUTEN-FREE

SERVES 4–6

8 garlic cloves

½" knob ginger

2–3 Thai green chilies

1½ teaspoons turmeric

¾ teaspoon chili powder

2 tablespoons canola oil, plus more for emulsifying paste

6 skinless chicken thighs, bone-in and room temperature

salt, to taste

2 cups chicken stock

1 (13½-ounce) can coconut milk

juice of ½ lemon

large handful of cilantro, finely chopped

1. To a small food processor, add the garlic, ginger, chilies, turmeric, and chili powder. Process until finely chopped and, with the food processor running, stream in a few tablespoons of oil until a fine paste forms.

2. Place the chicken thighs in a plastic bag and add half the garlic purée. Marinate for a minimum of 2 hours but preferably overnight. Reserve the other half.

3. Dry off the chicken thoroughly and season generously with salt. Heat a large sauté pan with high sides over medium-high heat. Add about 2 tablespoons of oil and sear the chicken thighs for 3 minutes on the first side and about 2 minutes on the other. Remove the chicken thighs and set aside. Reduce the heat to medium-low.

4. Add the remaining garlic purée and gently cook for 30 seconds. Add the chicken stock and nestle the thighs back in. Bring up to a boil and lower to a simmer. Simmer uncovered for about 10 minutes.

5. Add the coconut milk, flip the thighs, and bring back up to a simmer. Simmer for another 15 minutes, until the sauce has thickened and will coat a spoon. Add the lemon juice and cilantro. Taste and adjust the seasoning.

6. Serve hot over rice.

The Virtue of Fried Chicken

Like many other brides, on the night of my wedding celebration, I was young and foolish enough to wear some sort of tight-fitting ensemble that required weeks of calorie counting and potential malnourishment. I'm not quite sure whom I was trying to impress, but I'll just say it was an unnaturally skinny state of being for my body.

Needless to say, the morning after, once the dress had been worn, guests had been greeted, and photos had been taken, an uncontrollable hunger seized me, and I had to figure out which food was worthy of this momentous level of splurge. There was no doubt in my mind: fried chicken!

There is *nothing* better than biting into a salty, juicy, crispy piece of fried chicken. Nothing. With that first bite, as the crunchy texture of the crust gives way to that tender meat, I am a goner. I eat it in times of stress. I eat it in times of joy and celebration. I eat it in a proportion that makes zero sense for my size.

With that said, learning to make *my own fried chicken* has taken years of trials and tribulations, generally because it's not just *my own fried chicken*. The recipe I was seeking to create was for fried chicken that stops cravings with a single sitting, fried chicken that doesn't make me want to go out and have someone else's fried chicken, fried chicken that is in a class of its own.

And finally, after years, I achieved fried chicken nirvana. It's a bit of a science, and there are a few key steps:

- First, I brine the chicken in a rich buttermilk base with spices like saffron and aromatics like garlic. The brine has salt and sugar, which causes the chicken to absorb the spice-infused liquid, making it both juicy and flavorful.
- The brine also has a few eggs in it, which will ultimately help seal in the moisture, reduce oil absorption, and make the crust have a delicate crispness when you go to fry.

- Next, I double dip the chicken in the crust and the buttermilk marinade. This gives it a gorgeously thick and crisp crust that, again, seals in the moisture and keeps its crunchiness even when it's cold.
- Finally, perfect fry temperature is key. The chicken has to be cooked in 325°F oil for the entire time, so I start it a bit high since the temperature falls when the chicken is added.
- Follow these steps and you too will achieve fried chicken nirvana.

That day after my wedding, post-fried-chicken-gluttony, I couldn't move from a semi-reclined position for somewhere upwards of 5 hours—immobilized by a feeling of fullness, to put it mildly (and, to be more clear, sickness). I questioned my decision-making capabilities and, for once, lamented the extent of my fried chicken consumption. Unlike after tequila fiascos, however, I was undeterred. Fried chicken is still my splurge, and I love making it as much as I love eating it.

Saffron Fried Chicken

Saffron is used in a lot of Middle Eastern and South Asian marinades, oftentimes with yogurt, and I use it in my saffron buttermilk marinade here that also serves to brine the chicken and make it even juicier. I then double dip the chicken to create a super-crisp crust, and let it air-dry while the meat loses its chill. Finally, frying at the perfect temperature ensures fried chicken nirvana—crisp, flavorful, aromatic, tender, and juicy. Enjoy!

SERVES 4

1 (3- to 4-pound) broiler / fryer chicken, cut into 8 pieces
vegetable shortening or peanut oil, for frying

For the marinade / brine:
3 cups buttermilk, divided
very generous pinch saffron
2 eggs
3 garlic cloves, minced
½ teaspoon Dijon mustard
2 tablespoons salt
1 tablespoon sugar

For the crust:
1 cup all-purpose flour
½ cup cornstarch
1 teaspoon salt
1 teaspoon black pepper
1½ teaspoons granulated garlic
1½ teaspoons granulated onion
1 teaspoon sweet paprika
pinch cayenne pepper

1. In a small saucepan, heat ½ cup of the buttermilk over medium heat until it comes up to a bare simmer. Add saffron and switch off heat. Let it sit for 10 minutes.

2. Pour this mixture along with the remaining buttermilk and the rest of the marinade ingredients into a blender and blend on high until smooth. Place chicken in a bowl or casserole dish and cover with the marinade. Refrigerate for a minimum of 6 hours and up to 24.

3. In a large bowl, paper bag, or plastic bag, combine the crust ingredients thoroughly. Remove chicken from marinade and place in a colander for a few minutes to drain, reserving the marinade. Dredge or shake chicken pieces individually in the flour mixture and place on a wire rack fitted over a baking sheet.

4. Dip chicken once more in the marinade, letting any excess drip off. Coat again in the flour mixture and place back on the wire rack. Let chicken sit on the rack for an hour to dry and come up to room temperature.

5. In a large, heavy-bottomed pot, heat 3" to 4" of oil to 350°F for deep-frying. You actually want to fry the chicken at 325°F for the entire time, but the temperature will drop once you add it in. Place chicken in the hot oil and fry for 13 to 17 minutes, making sure the temperature stays at 325°F. I like to take the wings out at 13 minutes and fry the rest between 15 and 17 minutes, depending on the size of the pieces and the type of meat. White meat cooks faster than dark meat, and fatter pieces will cook more slowly. If the juices run clear, the chicken is cooked through.

6. Serve hot! It can be held uncovered in a 250°F oven to stay warm, but it's preferable to serve immediately.

Chicken Salad with Bacon, Walnuts, and Fruit

At first glance, this looks like it could be a traditional chicken salad, but the inspiration for this dish is Circassian Chicken, a Turkish dish in which poached chicken is shredded and combined with a walnut sauce. Here, instead of mayonnaise, toasted walnuts are spun in the food processor with pita soaked in milk to form the base. I added bacon and shallot for smoke and crunch, and the fruit adds a sweet, watery bite to the salad. This is fantastic in a sandwich or just by itself with some greens.

SERVES 4–6

2 tablespoons olive oil

3 slices bacon, cut into a fine dice

4 boneless, skinless chicken breasts

salt and freshly ground black pepper, to taste

1 piece of pita, plus more for serving

1 cup milk

2 cups walnuts, toasted (see sidebar)

2 garlic cloves

pinch chili flakes

1 shallot, minced

½ cup grape halves, pomegranate arils, or dried cranberries or cherries

small handful of cilantro, finely chopped

1. Preheat oven to 375°F.

2. Heat a large, ovensafe skillet over medium heat. Add the oil and the bacon and cook a few minutes until the bacon crisps and has rendered most of its fat. Use a slotted spoon to transfer the bacon bits to a paper towel–lined plate. Turn the heat up to medium-high.

3. Season the chicken breasts generously with salt and pepper and place carefully in the hot pan. Cook 3 minutes per side and then transfer to the oven. Finish in the oven for another 10 to 15 minutes. Cool breasts down and dice into bite-sized pieces.

4. Break up the piece of pita and place it in a bowl. Cover with the milk and let soak 5 to 10 minutes.

5. In a small food processor, process the walnuts until they are still coarse. You want to maintain texture and not completely powder the walnuts. Add the garlic cloves, chili flakes, and the soaked pita along with the milk. Process until a uniform paste. Season to taste.

6. Add the diced chicken and bacon to a large bowl. Throw in the walnut paste, shallot, fruit, and cilantro. Mix thoroughly and season to taste.

7. Chill in the refrigerator for at least an hour. Serve in pitas or on a bed of greens.

Toasting the walnuts is an incredibly important step and key to the flavor of the dish. You can do this in a pan or on a baking sheet in a 350°F oven for about 5 to 10 minutes.

Korean-Style BBQ Chicken or Turkey Drumsticks

These drumsticks are inspired by Korean barbecue—that perfect blend of sweet, salty, spicy, and umami. For that signature flavor, I use Gochujang, a sweet Korean chili sauce, which adds just the right heat here, but you can use another chili sauce like sriracha and still get great results. Easy to do in the oven, these require nothing more than a dip in a marinade that doubles as a glaze and some cook time. Cooking outdoors? These taste even better on the grill . . . .

SERVES 4–6

10–12 chicken drumsticks (approximately 3 pounds), or 5 to 6 small turkey drumsticks

1 tablespoon gochujang, sriracha, or other chili sauce (see sidebar)

4–6 garlic cloves, minced

½ teaspoon minced ginger

1 tablespoon mirin

½ cup low-sodium soy sauce

1 tablespoon sesame oil

2 teaspoons honey

toasted sesame seeds, to garnish

1. Place the chicken in a plastic bag and add the chili sauce, garlic, ginger, mirin, soy sauce, sesame oil, and honey. Close and turn to distribute the ingredients evenly. Marinate for a minimum of 6 hours or overnight.

2. Preheat the oven to 450°F.

3. Remove the drumsticks from the marinade, reserving the marinade, and wipe them dry. Place them on a baking sheet fitted with a rack and let them come up to room temperature. Place in the oven and drop the temperature to 375°F. Roast for 35 minutes for the chicken drumsticks, longer for the turkey, so that a thermometer registers 165°F when inserted.

4. While the drumsticks are cooking, strain the marinade into a saucepan. Bring up to a boil and reduce to a simmer. Simmer uncovered for 5 to 10 minutes, until the sauce coats a spoon and becomes a bit syrupy.

5. Serve drumsticks hot, brushed with the soy glaze and sprinkled with the toasted sesame seeds.

> If you are using a chili sauce other than gochujang, bump up the sweetness a bit— add another teaspoon of honey.

"Chicken and Biscuits"

Chicken and biscuits is a comfort classic, a rich stew topped with buttery biscuits. The flavor and texture is not unlike having a bite of chicken, stuffing, and gravy all at once! I took it a step further using a Provençal-style base for the chicken stew and infusing my cheddar-buttermilk biscuits with lovely Herbes de Provence. This dish is incredibly aromatic and satisfying and needs little more than a salad or some garlicky greens to be an entire meal. It's also great for entertaining since everything can be assembled ahead of time and baked off right before your guests arrive.

SERVES 4–6

For the chicken:
3 tablespoons olive oil
2 pounds chicken, boneless breasts and/or thighs, cut into stew pieces
salt and freshly ground black pepper
3 slices Jambon de Bayonne or Prosciutto, cut into a fine dice
½ pound porcini or shiitake mushrooms, thinly sliced
2 tablespoons unsalted butter
1 medium yellow onion, finely chopped
2 shallots, finely chopped
1 celery stalk, finely chopped
3–4 garlic cloves, minced
½ teaspoon fennel seeds
small bunch thyme
1 fresh or dried bay leaf
¼ cup white wine
¼ cup sweet fortified wine like Banyuls, Port, or Sherry
3 tablespoons all-purpose flour

2 cups chicken stock

¼ cup heavy cream

small handful parsley, finely chopped

For the biscuits:

2 cups all-purpose flour

2 teaspoons baking powder

½ teaspoon baking soda

1 teaspoon salt

¼ teaspoon black pepper

2 teaspoons Herbes de Provence

½ stick cold, unsalted butter, cut into small cubes + 1 tablespoon for brushing

¼ cup vegetable shortening, chilled and cut into small pieces

1½ cups grated Gruyère or Cheddar cheese

¾ cups cold buttermilk

kosher or Maldon salt

1. Preheat the oven to 425°F.

2. *For the chicken*: Heat a large sauté pan with straight sides over medium-high heat and add the olive oil. Season the chicken pieces with salt and pepper and add to the pan. Let brown in the pan for 2 minutes, then stir and sauté for another minute. You really want to develop color on the chicken, so work in batches if necessary so as not to overcrowd the pan. Remove to a plate.

3. Add the ham and mushrooms to the pan and let brown again for about 2 minutes. Add the butter, onion, shallots, and celery and a bit of salt to draw out the moisture and reduce the heat to medium. Cook for another 3 to 5 minutes until the onions are translucent. Add the minced garlic and sauté for another minute just until it's fragrant. Add the fennel seeds, thyme, bay leaf, and both of the wines and let reduce. Use a wooden spoon to scrape off any bits from the bottom of the pan.

4. Once all the wine has reduced, add the flour and stir to evenly incorporate. Add back in the chicken along with any accumulated juices and the stock and simmer partially covered for 10 minutes. Add the heavy cream and simmer uncovered for another 5 minutes. Add the parsley and stir to combine.

5. *For the biscuits*: In a food processor or stand mixer, sift the flour, baking powder, baking soda, salt, black pepper, and Herbes de Provence together. Add the half stick of cold, cubed butter, and the shortening and pulse or mix just until a sandy texture forms, and there are no visible clumps. Add the cheese and pulse to combine. Pour the buttermilk in all at once and pulse until the dough sticks together.

6. Turn the dough out onto a floured surface. Gently knead the dough a few times so that it comes together and forms into a flat, ½" thick disc. Use a 2" cutter to cut out a dozen biscuits.

7. Layer on top of the chicken stew, brush with remaining butter and sprinkle with a little flake salt. Bake for 15 to 20 minutes until golden brown.

The key to making tender, flaky biscuits is to not overdevelop the glutens in the dough. One way to do this is to keep all of the ingredients cold, and another is to not work the dough too much.

Baked Chicken with Chorizo, Fennel, and Green Olives

This chicken dish is inspired by flavors I tasted while in Barcelona, Spain. I love using this technique with the whole chicken or even just the thighs—first, a quick sear to crisp up the chicken skin and then a little double duty: the chicken juices flavor the sautéed vegetables and the vegetables infuse the chicken with moisture while they roast together. On a carb-light weeknight, I make a salad while the chicken is roasting and call it a day, but this is extra luxurious with some silky mashed potatoes topped with the chorizo and fennel.

SERVES 4–6

For the chicken:

1 whole (3- to 4-pound) chicken, cut into 8 pieces

⅓ cup all-purpose flour

1 tablespoon smoked Spanish paprika

2½ teaspoons cumin seeds, toasted then ground into a powder

2 teaspoons ground black pepper

¼ teaspoon cayenne pepper

pinch saffron

2½ teaspoons salt

1 teaspoon unsalted butter

2 teaspoons canola oil

For the chorizo and vegetables:

3 links chorizo, sliced

1 large yellow onion, thinly sliced

1 bulb fennel, thinly sliced, fronds reserved

2 garlic cloves, minced

¼ cup pitted green olives (manzanilla, cerignola), sliced

¼ cup raw, unsalted marcona almonds, toasted

1 teaspoon orange zest

1. Preheat the oven to 400°F and place the rack on the rung second from the top.

2. Let the chicken come up to room temperature. Mix together the flour with the smoked Spanish paprika, cumin, black pepper, cayenne, saffron, and salt. Dredge chicken pieces in the flour mixture and shake off any excess.

3. Heat a large (ovenproof) pan or cast-iron skillet over medium-high heat. Add butter and oil and when the foam subsides, place chicken pieces skin-side down in the pan. You may need to work in batches if the pan isn't big enough. Let the chicken cook for 3 to 4 minutes, until the skin turns crisp. Be careful not to let the heat creep up too high or the spices will burn. Flip and let cook another 2 minutes. Remove to a plate and set aside.

4. Reduce heat to medium and pour off excess oil. Add chorizo and let brown for 3 to 4 minutes. Remove using a slotted spoon to a plate and set aside. Add the onion and fennel with a bit more salt to draw out the moisture and cook for 5 to 7 minutes, until the onions are translucent and the vegetables have softened. Add the garlic and cook for another minute. Switch off heat and add the olives, almonds, and chorizo and toss to combine. Place the chicken pieces on top of the bed of vegetables and place in the oven. Cook for 25 to 30 minutes (until the juices run clear out of the chicken or a meat thermometer in the thigh registers about 165°F).

5. Serve chicken hot, sprinkled with the orange zest, with a side of the vegetables and garnished with fennel fronds.

The chicken should stay crisp, but this depends on how much moisture is coming off the vegetables. If you need to re-crisp the chicken, pop them back in a clean sauté pan, skin-side down, with a bit of oil for a minute over medium-high heat.

Universal BBQ

I've found one truth in all of my travels, all over the world: the existence of *universal BBQ*. Without fail, every place I've visited or even read about has it: typically outdoor cooking or smoking of meats over wood, charcoal, or gas. Grilling, roasting, spit-roasting, or broiling all count, and to my knowledge there isn't a country in the world that doesn't do it!

We can start with American barbecue, the much-beloved pastime that typically features sweet, sour, and salty flavors—the nuances within the continental United States are serious, and whether you are on the North Carolina or Memphis side can make or break a friendship.

In South America, there is Brazilian *churrasco* and the famed Peruvian *anticuchos*, skewered pieces of meat, typically calves' hearts, marinated in aji panca, vinegar, garlic, salt, and cumin that are char-grilled and heavenly. Anticuchos aren't too far off from Middle Eastern shish kebab or Indian seekh kebab, which are also tenderized and marinated for quite some time and excellent after a night of partying.

I've also had Afghani barbecue, which is similar to shish kebab but with much bigger pieces of meat—a tender, richly spiced food memory from my childhood that I can't forget. Korean barbecue has that perfect mix of heat, flavor, and sweetness, and the restaurants I frequent in NYC cook it right there in front of you. In parts of Africa, grilled meats are for celebrations or merely street food—in Kenya, *Nyama Choma* is a staple: freshly roasted, aromatic pieces of meat that serve to feed and bring people together. I am missing a host of countries and barbecue styles here because I can't possibly name them all.

The list can't go on without mentioning Jamaican Jerk, that spicy, smoky grilled chicken and meat that has become almost synonymous with the country. I was bowled over by the depth of flavor when I visited the country (see my take on it on the next page). In fact, several of my poultry recipes are BBQ-inspired: Jamaican Jerk Hens, Korean-Style Drumsticks, and the Brick Chicken. And why shouldn't they be? The flavor is tremendous, giving poultry that boost it needs to go from being simple to complex.

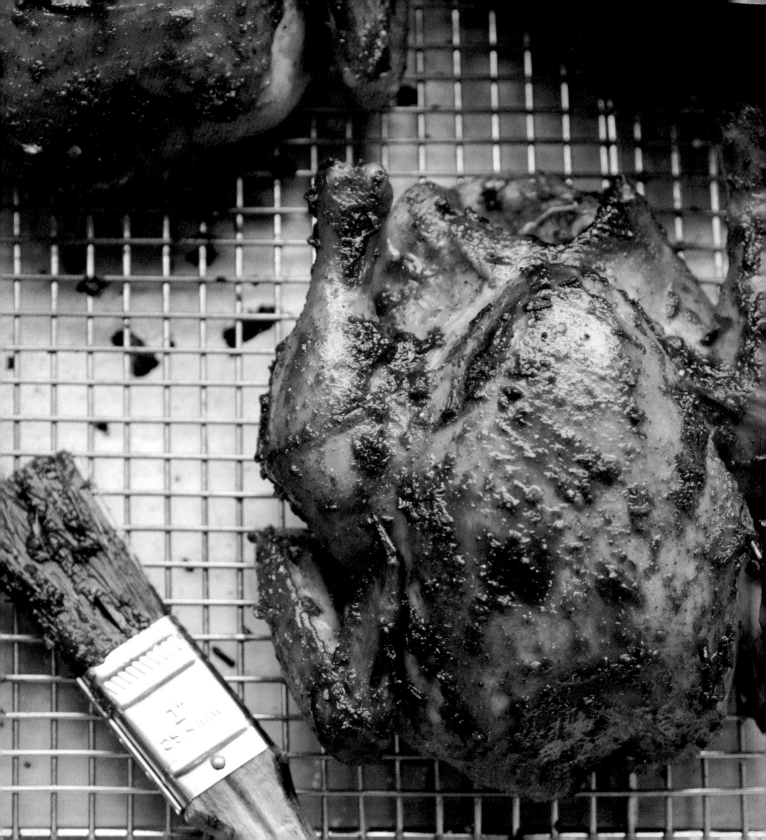

Jamaican Jerk Hens

Jamaican Jerk is a true barbecue tradition. I learned from a great chef in Montego Bay named Vincent and he showed me all the amazing ingredients he uses to make his jerk. Although I love the seasoning on ribs or other meats, I think poultry with that crisp, glazed skin is the best medium to show off this style of cooking. I chose Cornish hens here because they are individually sized and an impressive dinner item, but the marinade is the same if you want to choose a different bird. In the summer, I'd use a charcoal grill sprinkled with allspice berries or with some smoldering wood to get a smokier flavor, but these are still delicious done right in the oven.

SERVES 4

4 Cornish hens (approximately 1½ pounds each), rinsed and patted dry

For the jerk marinade:

12 garlic cloves

2–3 Scotch bonnet peppers

1 medium yellow onion, quartered

1" knob ginger

2 green onions, white and light green parts only

3 teaspoons fresh thyme leaves

1 teaspoon ground allspice

1 teaspoon ground black pepper

1 dried bay leaf, crushed

½ teaspoon ground cinnamon

2 tablespoons brown sugar

6 tablespoons soy sauce

1 teaspoon Worcestershire sauce

For the jerk sauce:
4 tablespoons coconut or canola oil
2 tablespoons honey
¼ cup pineapple juice
salt, to taste

1. Place the Cornish hens in plastic bags. To a small food processor, add the garlic, peppers, onion, ginger, and green onion and pulse to finely chop. Add in the remaining marinade ingredients and process until finely puréed. Transfer half the marinade to a small saucepan and divide the remaining marinade between the Cornish hens. Marinate for a minimum of 2 hours, preferably overnight.

2. To the remaining marinade in the saucepan, add the oil, honey, and pineapple juice and simmer uncovered over medium heat for 5 to 7 minutes, until the sauce thickens and becomes like a glaze. Taste and adjust seasoning and set aside. We'll use this jerk glaze to baste the hens while they are cooking.

3. Remove the hens from the marinade, then wipe clean and discard the marinade. You want them to be dry. Let them sit out on a rack on a baking sheet for about 45 minutes to come to room temperature. Preheat the oven to 425°F.

4. Season the hens all over and inside their cavity with salt. Make sure they are breast-side up on the rack and place them in the oven. Let them roast for 15 minutes and then reduce the heat to 375°F for another 10 minutes. Brush with the jerk glaze all over and return to the oven for another 10 to 15 minutes, until they are cooked through, the juices run clear, and a meat thermometer inserted into the thigh registers 165°F.

5. Let the hens rest for about 5 to 10 minutes, loosely tented with foil, before serving. Serve with any remaining jerk sauce on the side.

In Jamaica, in order to impart that signature sweet smokiness to their jerk dishes, cooks use the wood of the *pimento* (or the allspice tree). They may also line the inside of the grill with cinnamon leaves to smolder and infuse the dishes.

Moroccan Chicken Pie

The inspiration for this dish comes from two very different places: (1) Bastilla—a Moroccan pigeon pie that's made with layers of phyllo dough, tons of eggs and spices, and braised, shredded pigeon—and (2) a few chicken pie recipes from Clementine Paddleford's The Great American Cookbook *(great read!). I wanted the flavor of bastilla with a slightly shorter prep and cooking time and the feel of an old-fashioned chicken pie. That is what I think we have here—fragrant with spices, with incredible texture from the nuts, and a flaky crust courtesy of store-bought puff pastry.*

YIELDS 1 (9½") PIE

For the chicken filling:

3 tablespoons unsalted butter

1 shallot, finely chopped

1 medium leek, white and light green parts only, thinly sliced

¼ fennel bulb, finely chopped

¼ teaspoon minced ginger

1½ pounds ground chicken

3 garlic cloves, minced

½ teaspoon ground cinnamon

¼ teaspoon ground allspice

¾ teaspoon turmeric

1 teaspoon ground coriander

1 teaspoon ground black pepper

pinch cayenne

pinch saffron

1 dry bay leaf, crushed

½ cup chicken stock

salt and freshly ground black pepper, to taste

¼ teaspoon lemon zest

small handful of fresh cilantro, finely chopped

7 eggs, divided

½ cup heavy cream, plus extra for the egg wash

salt and freshly ground black pepper

For the nuts:

½ cup unsalted marcona almonds, toasted

2 tablespoons sugar

½ teaspoon ground cinnamon

For the crust:

2 sheets of puff pastry, thawed per package instructions

confectioners' sugar, for dusting

1. Preheat the oven to 400°F.

2. Heat a large sauté pan with straight sides over medium heat. Add the butter and when the foam subsides, toss in the shallot, leek, fennel, ginger, and a bit of salt to draw out the moisture. Cook for 4 to 6 minutes, until the vegetables have softened and the shallot is translucent.

3. Turn the heat to medium-high and add the chicken, garlic, spices, and bay leaf. Cook for 2 to 3 minutes, using a wooden spoon to break up the meat. Add the chicken stock and when it simmers, reduce the heat and simmer partially covered for 20 minutes, until the chicken is cooked through and the spices have penetrated. Remove from the heat, season generously to taste with salt and pepper, and let cool until it's just warm to the touch. Add in the lemon zest and chopped cilantro.

4. Separate 2 of the eggs (reserving the whites for later use in another recipe, if desired), and in a large bowl, beat 4 of the eggs along with the 2 yolks. Add the heavy cream and season generously. Using a slotted spoon, transfer the chicken mixture into the egg mixture and combine thoroughly.

5. To the bowl of a food processor, add the toasted almonds, sugar, and cinnamon and process until it forms a coarse meal.

6. Roll out the 2 sheets of puff pastry on a lightly floured surface so that they are larger than your 9½" pie dish. Place the pie dish on a baking sheet and drape one sheet of rolled out puff pastry in the pie dish, letting the ends hang off the sides. Sprinkle half of the almond mixture in the bottom of the pie dish, fill with the chicken mixture, and top with the other half of the almond mixture. Place the other rolled-out puff pastry sheet on top, cut the over-hang with a paring knife, and crimp the edges together decoratively.

7. Beat together the remaining egg with a bit of heavy cream to make an egg wash and brush the surface of the pastry all over with the egg wash. Cut slits in the top of the pie to let out steam and place the baking sheet in the oven. Bake for 30 to 40 minutes, until the crust is golden.

8. Remove from the oven and let cool briefly. Dust with confectioners' sugar, if desired, before serving.

Crispy, Brick Chicken Thighs with Roasted Garlic and Sweet Lemon-Ginger Confit

My mom used to make this delicious lemon chicken growing up, breasts pounded thin in a rich, lemon pan sauce, and I thought I'd riff on that here. I changed the technique to cooking the chicken under a brick for foolproof crackling-crisp chicken skin and made it a dry version, using lemon confit in lieu of making a sauce. Lemon confit is a means of preserving lemons, poaching lemon slices in oil until they become jamlike, and this recipe is easy, tasty, and adds the perfect musky citrus flavor to the crisp thighs. GLUTEN-FREE

SERVES 4–6

For the confit:

1 lemon, sliced and seeded

¾ cup canola or olive oil

½" knob ginger, roughly chopped

pinch chili flakes

1 bay leaf

1 teaspoon honey

For the chicken:

2 pounds chicken thighs, skin-on with bone (4–6 thighs)

2–3 tablespoons unsalted butter, softened at room temperature

4–6 cloves Roasted Garlic (see Chapter 1)

2–3 tablespoons canola oil

salt and freshly ground black pepper, to taste

1. *For the confit:* Add all the ingredients to a small saucepan and place uncovered over medium-high heat. When it starts to bubble, reduce the heat to a very low simmer and let simmer uncovered for 1 to 1½ hours. The lemon slices should become soft and almost jamlike, but you want them to still keep their shape. Let cool completely, drain lemon slices of excess oil, reserving it. Remove the ginger and bay leaf and pat dry.

2. *For the chicken:* Dry the chicken thighs thoroughly. Under the skin of each thigh, place a ½ lemon confit slice, ½ tablespoon of the butter, and 1 clove of roasted garlic. Massage in underneath the skin. Drizzle oil over both sides of the thighs and season generously with salt and freshly ground black pepper.

3. Place a large cast-iron skillet over medium-high heat. When hot, add oil just to thinly coat the bottom of the skillet and add the chicken thighs skin-side down. Place another, foil-wrapped skillet of equal size on top and weigh it down with bricks or cans. Reduce the heat to medium-low and let cook for 15 minutes. Remove the weighted pan and check the thighs from time to time to make sure the skin is getting evenly cooked.

4. Remove the weighted pan, flip the thighs, and finish cooking for another 3 to 5 minutes (until the juices run clear out of the chicken or a meat thermometer in the thigh registers about 165°F).

5. Serve hot with the sides of your choice!

Lemon confit is a way of preserving lemons. If you have any lemon slices left over at the end, you can store them covered in the oil for about a month in the fridge.

Chapter 6

BEEF, PORK, LAMB, AND GOAT

Truth be told, I could never be a vegetarian—I am a meat lover! In this section, I included some cultural classics from my travels like South African bobotie, Greek patsitsio, and Brazilian feijoada. These are dishes that I adore in their original form and have only minimally tweaked (I can't help myself). To balance these out, I wanted to showcase some of the twists I do at home: a pasta with a ragu made from West Indian–style braised oxtail, my take on a North African lamb tagine with seasonal butternut squash and apples, and a short rib chili made deeply aromatic with Ethiopian spices.

In all the dishes, technique plays a big part. I'm a huge fan of long braises to take cheaper, tougher cuts and turn them into something you can eat with a spoon. I've also mastered my rib technique, and my Espresso-Chipotle St. Louis–Style Spare Ribs compete with a pitmaster's.

All these recipes are big on flavor, so I dedicate this chapter to all my fellow meat lovers.

153

Espresso-Chipotle St. Louis–Style Spare Ribs

I am a rib gal, and this is hands-down my favorite way to make them. The dry rub acts like a cure, tenderizing the meat and making sure the ribs stay juicy, and is full of great spices—smoked Spanish paprika, cumin, and a touch of espresso powder. Slow-cooking them sealed in foil keeps in all of the flavor and juices, and the finish, the chipotle glaze, has the perfect balance of heat, sweetness from the honey, and that hint of coffee-bitterness. These are smoky, sweet, and deeply flavorful and will become a staple in your household. GLUTEN-FREE

SERVES 4–6

2 racks St. Louis–style spare ribs or baby back ribs (3 to 4 pounds), trimmed of excess fat and membranes

For the dry rub:

1 tablespoon smoked Spanish paprika

2 teaspoons brown sugar

2 teaspoons salt

1½ teaspoons granulated garlic

1 teaspoon black pepper

½ teaspoon ground cumin

½ teaspoon instant espresso powder

For the chipotle glaze:

½ (7-ounce) can chipotle in adobo (approximately 2–3 chipotles plus 2 tablespoons adobo sauce)

⅓ cup honey

¼ teaspoon instant espresso powder

1. Place the ribs on aluminum foil sheets long enough to cover them, meat-side up. In a small bowl, mix together the dry rub ingredients until uniform. Divide the dry rub between the two racks, rubbing into the meat side first and then flipping and rubbing into the bone side. Keep the racks meat-side down and seal the foil pouch tightly. Refrigerate overnight.

2. Preheat oven to 350°F.

3. Place both foiled racks (meat-side down) on a baking sheet and into the oven for 2 to 2½ hours. The meat should be fork tender and just short of falling off the bone.

4. In a blender, purée the chipotles with their sauce, the honey, and the espresso powder. Transfer to a small saucepan, set over medium-high heat, bring up to a strong bubble, and then remove from the heat. This glaze can get pretty spicy, particularly if you're multiplying this recipe, so make sure to taste it at this stage. You can always add more honey to balance out the heat for your own tastes or even dilute with some ketchup.

5. Remove the racks from the foil and brush all sides with the chipotle glaze. You can either finish these under the broiler or on a medium-high preheated grill for 3 to 5 minutes.

6. Serve hot with any remaining glaze.

So you only used half a can of chipotle in adobo here . . . what can you do with the rest? Purée and add it to a chicken marinade, use as a sauce for shrimp tacos, fold into mashed potatoes or mayonnaise for a quick and spicy condiment, add to your mac 'n' cheese, or mix in with butter to top corn or other veggies. Endless possibilities!

Honey-Braised Lamb Shanks with Butternut Squash and Apples

This lamb dish is based on North African tagines, which slow-braise lamb and other meats with both sweet and salty elements. While many tagines feature apricots, prunes, or raisins, I thought seasonal butternut squash and apples would provide the perfect sweet counterbalance to the spiced braise. I use lamb shank here because I love the flavor and the end result—spoonable, fall-off-the-bone meat in a rich stew. GLUTEN-FREE

SERVES 4

2–3 tablespoons canola oil

2½ pounds lamb shanks (approximately 2 shanks), room temperature

salt and freshly ground black pepper, to taste

1 large yellow onion, chopped

4 garlic cloves, minced

½ teaspoon ground ginger

large pinch saffron

1½ teaspoons cinnamon

4 cups beef or chicken stock

1 tablespoon honey

2 cups butternut squash, cut into a ¾" dice

1½ cups Honeycrisp or Fuji apples, cut into a ¾" dice

¼ cup sliced almonds, toasted, divided

1½ teaspoons sesame seeds, toasted

1. Preheat the oven to 325°F.

2. Heat a Dutch oven or large pot over medium-high heat. Add the oil, season the shanks generously with salt and freshly ground black pepper, and sear 2 to 3 minutes per side to develop a nice brown. Remove to a plate and reduce the heat to medium-low.

3. Add the onion and a bit of salt and sauté for 5 to 7 minutes, until the onions are translucent. Add the garlic, ginger, saffron, and cinnamon and sauté for another 30 seconds to a minute, until fragrant. Nestle the lamb shanks back in the pot and add in the stock and the honey. Cover, bring up to a boil, and then place in the oven.

4. Cook for 2 hours and 15 minutes and then remove from the oven. Toss in the squash, apples, and half of the almonds. Cover and put back in the oven for the next 45 minutes to an hour. The meat should be spoonable, basically falling off the bone.

5. Serve hot, garnished with the remaining almonds and sesame seeds. This is great alongside couscous.

My Feijoada

Feijoada is the national dish of Brazil, a rich and hearty stew with different types of meats, sausage, and black turtle beans. It's a dish that's cooked throughout the former Portuguese colonies like Angola, Mozambique, and even Goa (in India). It's smoky with a touch of heat and is a perfect winter dish. In Brazil, feijoada is usually served with rice, farofa (coarse cassava flour cooked in bacon fat), and orange wedges. The oranges give the right sharpness and acidity to offset the major flavors of the different meats. If you need to make a faster version of this recipe, soak the beans overnight, replace the pork shoulder and ham hock with smoked pork chops, and you can do this in an hour!

GLUTEN-FREE

SERVES 8–10

3 tablespoons canola oil

1 pound pork shoulder, cut into stew pieces

salt and freshly ground black pepper, to taste

½ pound chorizo links, cut into ½" rounds

½ pound linguica, Andouille, or other smoked sausage links, cut into ½" rounds

4 slices of bacon, cut into a fine dice

2 medium yellow onions, roughly chopped

4–5 garlic cloves, minced

⅔ pound corned beef, cut into 1" pieces

1 smoked ham hock

1 pig's ear, rinsed thoroughly (optional)

1 pound dry black turtle beans, rinsed, stones and dirt removed

6 cups chicken stock

2 fresh or dried bay leaves

1 small bunch of thyme

pinch chili flakes

segmented oranges and cooked rice, for garnish

1. Preheat oven to 325°F.

2. Heat a Dutch oven over medium-high heat and add canola oil. Season pork shoulder with salt and pepper and brown. Remove and set aside. In the same pot, brown sausages and bacon separately and set aside as well.

3. Reduce the heat to medium-low and add onions to the same pot. Sauté for 5 to 7 minutes, until translucent, add garlic, and cook for another 1 to 2 minutes. Add back in the seared meats, corned beef, ham hock, pig's ear if using, beans, stock, bay leaves, thyme, and chili flakes. Bring to boil and reduce to simmer. Cook for 30 minutes uncovered on the stovetop—skimming the scum from the top.

4. Cover and place into oven and cook for another 2½ hours. Remove from the oven and spoon 2 to 3 ladles of the beans into a bowl. Mash with a fork or the back of a spoon to make a paste. Return to stew.

5. Remove ham hock and cut away layer of fat to expose the meat. Shred meat and place back into soup.

6. Finally, remove the bay leaves and the thyme bundle. Adjust seasoning as needed, to taste.

7. Serve with rice and garnish with orange segments.

Cowboy Steak with Tellicherry Peppercorns and Balsamic– Red Onion Marmalade

Rib eye is by far my favorite cut of beef—the rich marbling and flavor are just what I crave when I want a serious steak. A cowboy steak is an extra-thick cut of rib eye with the bone frenched, presumably so you can grab it by the "handle" when you're eating. This steak doesn't need much to shine but is complemented by a nice crust of Tellicherry peppercorns and red onions cooked down with balsamic vinegar to a jamlike texture.

SERVES 4–6

For the red onion marmalade:
2–3 tablespoons olive oil
2–3 medium red onions, thinly sliced
salt to taste
1 generous pinch chili flakes
1 tablespoon sugar
¼ cup balsamic vinegar
2 tablespoons sweet fortified wine like Banyuls, Port, or Sherry

For the cowboy steak:
2 (2"–2½") bone-in rib eye steaks (2–2½ pounds each)
salt and coarsely ground Tellicherry peppercorn
2 tablespoons canola oil

1. *For the red onion marmalade:* Heat a large sauté pan with straight sides over medium heat. When it's hot, add the olive oil followed by the sliced red onions, some salt, and the chili flakes. Toss together and let cook about 15 minutes, stirring at intervals to make sure the onions are cooking evenly.

2. Add the sugar, balsamic vinegar, and wine and let cook for another 25 to 35 minutes until the onions are soft and jamlike.

3. *For the steaks:* Let the steaks sit out for 45 minutes to an hour to come up to room temperature and preheat the oven to 450°F. Heavily season all sides of the steak with salt and form a light crust with the coarsely ground Tellicherry peppercorn.

4. Heat a cast-iron skillet over medium-high heat or preheat the grill. If using the skillet, add the canola oil and the steaks. Cook 4 to 5 minutes per side and then transfer into the oven for another 10 to 15 minutes for medium rare. You can do the same on the grill, moving the steaks after searing to the indirect heat and covering the grill for the last 10 to 15 minutes of cooking.

5. Let the steaks rest about 10 minutes before serving. Serve with a warm spoonful of the Balsamic–Red Onion marmalade.

How to Make Browning

If you've ever had West Indian stewed chicken or oxtail, the foundation of it was probably browning. So what *is* browning? It's basically deeply caramelized sugar that starts a dish off—enhancing both the color and flavor of a dish, coating the rest of the ingredients with a touch of sweetness. Brown sugar is heated with a little oil until it caramelizes, starts to smoke, and turns really dark. At that point, water is added or ingredients are tossed in to stop the cooking process. Once the sugar is cooked to that stage, it develops a really rich flavor, molasses-like with smokiness and depth. It's great for stews, but it's also a key ingredient in West Indian black cake, a boozy, wine-soaked fruitcake that's served around the holidays.

You can find bottled browning, and I've found it at a number of West Indian and ethnic grocers. But the reality is that it is *really* easy to do at home, and I've used it in a few dishes here in the book—the Pappardelle with West Indian Stewed Oxtail Ragu and Gran's Peas and Rice. So I want to walk you through it step by step:

1. Start with a nice, thick-bottomed pot that retains heat well. If you are using the browning for a stew, this is the best vessel.
2. Heat the oil over medium heat. You want it to shimmer but not smoke.
3. Add in your brown sugar. You can use dark, light, or even palm sugar here.
4. Use a wooden spoon to start to "dissolve" the sugar in the oil. It will look sandy and wet at first.
5. Keep stirring and you should notice that the sugar will start to stick together and look straggly.
6. The next stage is when the sugar will liquefy and the oil will start smoking. Stop now! At this point the browning is made, and you should reduce the heat and add in the next ingredients.

The key with browning is taking it to the right stage. Any further and the sugar will completely burn and turn your whole dish bitter! (I know . . . sadly from experience.) You want it just short of burning.

Also, a word to the wise—browning is hot, temperature-wise! Never attempt to touch it or taste it, and be sure to stand back and gingerly add in your ingredients so you don't get spattered . . . .

Pappardelle with West Indian Stewed Oxtail Ragu

Patience is truly a virtue in cooking, and for me, oxtail is worth the wait. This muscle-y meat requires long, slow love to give up the goods and then falls completely and utterly off the bone. The bones and marrow have an incredibly robust beef flavor and make incredible stock. West Indian–style stewed oxtail has long been a favorite of mine, as it's delicious and oxtail is cheap! If you can't easily find oxtail, however, this would work beautifully with short ribs, shanks, or even pork shoulder or belly. It's traditionally eaten with peas and rice or even white rice, but it dawned on me one day just how good this stew would taste as a ragu for pasta. And voilà! This recipe was created.

SERVES 4–6

2½ pounds oxtail, cut into segments

salt and freshly ground black pepper, to taste

3 tablespoons canola oil

2½ tablespoons brown or palm sugar

2 medium yellow onions, roughly chopped

2 green onions, white and light green parts only, roughly chopped

1 jalapeño, roughly chopped

½ teaspoon minced ginger

4–5 garlic cloves, minced

1 quart beef stock

4–5 dashes of Worcestershire sauce

1 fresh or dried bay leaf

1 small bunch of thyme

2 tablespoons cilantro, finely chopped
1 pound fresh or dried pasta
chives or other fresh herbs, for garnish

1. Preheat the oven to 325°F. Let the oxtail come up to room temperature and season all sides generously with salt and pepper.

2. Heat a Dutch oven or heavy-bottomed pan over medium-high heat. Add the oil and when it shimmers, add in the oxtail pieces. Brown for about 2 minutes per side and remove to a plate.

3. Reduce heat to medium-low and add the sugar. (If the oil is heavily smoking, pull the pot off the heat for a minute or two to cool—if it's too hot the sugar will burn quickly.) Stir the sugar and once it has caramelized and starts to smoke (see instructions in *How to Make Browning* in this chapter), throw in the onions, jalapeño, ginger, and a bit of salt to draw out the moisture. Sauté for 5 to 7 minutes, until the onions turn translucent.

4. Add the minced garlic and sauté for another 30 seconds to a minute, just until it becomes fragrant. Now, add the beef stock, Worcestershire, bay leaf, thyme, and cilantro. Nestle the oxtail back into the pot, cover, and bring up to a boil. As soon as it boils, remove from the heat and put it into the oven, making sure it's covered tightly. Let it braise in there for 3 to 3½ hours, until the meat is fork tender and falling off the bone.

5. At this point, skim off as much of the oil/fat from the braising liquid as possible. I personally like to do this a day ahead and refrigerate. It's always better for the meat to cool in the braising liquid to keep its moisture, and the fat rises to the top of the liquid and solidifies. Then, it's really easy to skim it off.

6. Remove the oxtail pieces, using a ladle or spoon to take out as much as possible. Remove and discard the bay leaf and the thyme stems, and pour the remaining braising liquid along with the cooked-down onions, etc., into a food processor. Process until completely puréed and pour back into a clean pot. If it's nice and thick, you're good and you can keep it on low to warm through—if it's a bit watery, heat over medium-low and simmer uncovered for anywhere between 3 and 10 minutes to get it to a nice, thick ragu consistency.

7. Using a fork, remove the meat from the oxtail bones, making sure to discard any parts you deem too fatty. If the pieces are too big, chop with a knife to achieve bite-sized pieces. Return the oxtail meat to the saucepot and warm through.

8. Bring a large pot of water up to a boil and season generously with salt until the water tastes salty. Add the pasta and cook until al dente. Using a strainer or tongs, transfer the pasta directly into the oxtail ragu and add a ladleful of the starchy water as well.

9. Toss until the sauce and meat is evenly distributed and serve immediately, garnished with chives or any other fresh herbs you prefer.

Pork Chops with West African Tsire and Pan Gravy

A fragrant spice and nut blend called tsire is what I use to coat pork chops almost like bread crumbs here. Throughout West Africa, this blend is used on different meats before grilling and can be found at street food carts. A quick sear, and while the pork finishes in the oven, I make an elegant pan gravy from the drippings, some white wine, a touch of honey, butter, and thyme.

SERVES 4

4 pork rib chops, frenched (trim and scrape around the bone to expose it)

½ cup West African Tsire (see Chapter 1)

salt and freshly ground black pepper, to taste

3 tablespoons canola oil

4 tablespoons unsalted butter, divided

3 garlic cloves, minced

¼ cup white wine

½ cup chicken stock

½ teaspoon honey

½ teaspoon fresh thyme, finely chopped

1. Preheat oven to 350°F.

2. To tenderize the pork, place chops between sheets of plastic wrap and use a mallet to pound them out a bit. You don't want them super thin, just to about a ½" thick.

3. Dredge chops on all sides in the tsire, pressing the blend in to stick, and season generously with salt and freshly ground black pepper. Heat a large skillet over medium-high heat. Add the oil and 2 tablespoons of butter. When the foam subsides, add the chops. Cook them 2 minutes per side, then transfer to a baking sheet. Work in batches so you don't crowd the pan and then finish in the oven for 5 minutes while you're making the pan sauce.

4. Pour off any excess oil, reduce the heat to medium, and add the minced garlic to the pan. Cook for 30 seconds to a minute and then add the white wine, scraping up any bits from the bottom of the pan. When the wine has reduced by ⅔, add the chicken stock and honey. Cook for another 3 to 4 minutes, until it has reduced by half. Remove from the heat and stir in the remaining 2 tablespoons of butter and the fresh thyme.

5. Let chops rest 5 minutes under a foil tent before serving. Serve with a bit of pan gravy spooned on top.

Smoky Lamb Meatballs

These meatballs prep up pretty quickly and make an easy weeknight meal (especially if you freeze them), paired with some salad, sautéed greens, or even a garlic and olive oil pasta. I use two secret ingredients here to achieve smokiness. The first, black cardamom, is used throughout North and East African cooking, in South Asian and Middle Eastern cuisine, and even in Sichuan cooking. It has a darker, woodsier flavor than green cardamom and pairs beautifully with lamb. The other, smoked Spanish paprika, is a staple in my spice pantry—it imparts great smokiness without heat. Enjoy!

SERVES 6–8 (YIELDS 60 1¼" MEATBALLS)

2 tablespoons unsalted butter

1 tablespoon olive oil, plus extra to coat pan

3 shallots, finely chopped

5–6 garlic cloves, minced

2 pounds ground lamb, room temperature

1 cup plain bread crumbs

2 egg yolks

2½ teaspoons ground black cardamom (see sidebar)

2 teaspoons ground black pepper

2 teaspoons chili powder

1 tablespoon smoked Spanish paprika

1 tablespoon salt

1. Preheat oven to 375°F.

2. Heat a small skillet over medium heat. Add the butter and 1 tablespoon of olive oil. When the foam subsides, add the shallot and garlic and sauté for 3 to 4 minutes, until the shallots are translucent. Set aside to cool.

3. To a large mixing bowl, add the ground lamb and make a well in the center. Add the cooled shallot/garlic mixture and the rest of the ingredients. Carefully mix to ensure even distribution. I like to make a claw with my hands and fold over the meat mixture repeatedly. You don't want to mash or overmix because it will make the meatballs tough.

4. Using wet hands, roll even-sized pieces of the mixture into balls. I make my meatballs about 1¼" in diameter, so if you make yours larger or smaller, adjust the cooking time appropriately.

5. Heat a large skillet over medium-high heat. When it's hot, add olive oil to coat the bottom of the pan and place meat-balls into the pan. These brown pretty quickly, so I cook for about 30 seconds to a minute on each side. Work in batches so you don't overcrowd the pan (you want browned meatballs, not steamed), and place browned meatballs in a baking dish.

6. Once all the meatballs have been browned, cover the baking dish with foil and place it in the oven. Bake for 20 to 25 minutes, until cooked through, firm, but tender.

7. Serve warm alongside your favorite dipping sauce.

Black cardamom are the darker cousins of the green sort and have a smokier flavor to them—great for lamb. I use my spice grinder to grind the whole pods of black cardamom, and then I pass it through a fine mesh sieve to get rid of the coarse bits. If you only have green cardamom on hand, that works too; it's still delicious.

Short Rib Chili with Ethiopian Spices

I learned how to make authentic Ethiopian dishes at a little restaurant in Brooklyn. Berbere, a signature Ethiopian dried spice blend that includes spices and herbs like dried chilies, garlic, ginger, red onion, and sacred basil, has become a staple in my pantry. Sprinkled on lamb chops before they hit the grill, on burgers, or as part of this chili, the flavor is rich and round and complements hearty meats. This chili is fragrant and spiced, and I love the textural difference of the shredded short ribs and ground beef.

SERVES 6–8

1½ pounds bone-in short-rib

salt and freshly ground black pepper, to taste

2–3 tablespoons canola oil

2 pounds ground beef

1 large yellow onion, finely chopped

1 shallot, finely chopped

1 jalapeño, finely chopped

4–5 garlic cloves, minced

2 teaspoons tomato paste

¼ cup Berbere

6 cups chicken stock

1 fresh or dried bay leaf

1 (28-ounce) can of crushed tomatoes

¼ cup cider vinegar

2 tablespoons dark brown sugar

1 pound dried red kidney beans, soaked overnight and drained

crème fraîche or sour cream, for garnish

1. Preheat the oven to 325°F.

2. Heat a Dutch oven over medium-high heat. Season short ribs all over with salt and freshly ground black pepper. Add oil to the pot and sear the short ribs for 2 minutes per side to get a nice brown on them. Work in batches if necessary so as not to overcrowd the pot and then remove them to a plate once seared.

3. Add ground beef to the Dutch oven and let brown for 3 to 4 minutes. Reduce heat to medium-low and add onions, shallots, jalapeño, and a bit of salt to draw out the moisture. Sauté for another 5 minutes, until the onions are translucent, and then add in the minced garlic, tomato paste, and Berbere. Cook for another 30 seconds to a minute, until the garlic is fragrant.

4. Add the stock, bay leaf, and the short ribs along with any accumulated juices back into the pot. Cover, bring up to a boil, and place in the oven to cook for an hour.

5. After an hour, remove from the oven and stir in the crushed tomatoes, vinegar, dark brown sugar, and kidney beans. Cover, place back in the oven, and cook for another 2 hours.

6. After 2 hours, let the cover partially open and cook for another hour to thicken up for a total of 4 hours cooking time. Remove the short ribs, shred the meat, discard the bone, and return the meat to the chili. Season to taste.

7. Serve hot with a dollop of crème fraîche or sour cream.

Roasted Marrow Bones with Garlic and Herbed Bread Crumbs

Growing up, there was always a fight amongst the younger generation in my family for the marrow bones in the stews and curries during big family gatherings. We had marrow spoons, and, for me, spooning up spiced marrow was one of the best parts of the meal. Marrow isn't eaten as widely in the Western world, but it's incredibly nutrient dense, tasty, and inexpensive—a great way to use up leftover parts. Here, roasted with garlic, bread crumbs, and fresh herbs, the flavor is salty and nutty, and the bread crumbs impart a texture that works for even the marrow-squeamish.

SERVES 4

2–3 pounds center-cut beef marrow bones

4 garlic cloves, minced

¾ teaspoon chili flakes

¾ teaspoon sherry vinegar

¼ cup bread crumbs

1½ tablespoons chopped fresh herbs (chives, thyme, parsley, etc.)

salt to taste

canola oil

1. Preheat oven to 450°F.

2. Let the bones sit out for about 10 to 15 minutes to get closer to room temperature. Using a small pairing knife, run your knife along the edges of the marrow on both sides of the bones. You should be able to pop out the marrows.

3. Finely chop the marrow and add to a medium bowl. Add the garlic, chili flakes, sherry vinegar, bread crumbs, and herbs and season with a bit of salt. Mix to a uniform consistency.

4. Rub the outsides of the bones with oil and place on a foil-lined baking sheet. Make sure the baking sheet has a lip on it—some of the fat will leak out as the bones are cooking.

5. Place the marrow mixture back in the bones, stuffing to completely fill, and pile it a bit higher on the top so you can use all the mixture. Roast for 15 minutes.

6. Serve hot by themselves, with a small side salad, or with toasted bread for spreading.

A Lesson in South African Cookery

I still remember that night and that drive through the mountains to get to Kalk Bay in Cape Town. The skies had opened up and had this almost surreal quality to them, clouds fit for a water-color or postapocalyptic movie. We were driving for some time, and all of a sudden we rounded the bend, and there we were at the edge of a fishing village, one of the oldest in all of South Africa. We slowly climbed up to our destination, a little home tucked right into the mountain.

Gertie was the lady of the house and welcomed me in. Warm and effusive, she quickly ushered me into the kitchen, and we were aproned up, chatting and chopping like old friends in no time. She had a full menu to teach me, and my eyes and ears were wide open, trying to absorb all of the nuances this cuisine has to offer. South African culture is truly multiethnic, a rich combination of all of the peoples that have immigrated to and inhabited the country—Dutch, Malay, Indian, Arab, Portuguese, German, and of course the indigenous Africans (Khoikhoi, Xhosa, Zulu). We cooked up a feast!

- A beautiful squid and mussel salad, from the Cape's southeast and west coasts.
- South Africa's "crayfish," also known as spiny or rock lobster, spice-marinated and grilled.
- Rack of lamb from the Karoo region, a semi-desert area of the country where the bush diet imparts incredible flavor to the meat.
- Vegetable daal, a gorgeous lentil dish with Indian origins.
- Cape Malva pudding—a seminal dessert of South Africa with both Dutch and Malay origins.
- And my favorite dish of the night: bobotie.

Gertie's family was of Dutch descent, but she, a veteran of the food business, was also incredibly knowledgeable about Cape Malay food. Cape Malay people are a community of Muslim, Malaysian heritage that arrived in South Africa from Java in the 1600s. Their food has become synonymous with South African cuisine. Bobotie is a Cape Malay dish and classically South African. It's a layered casserole of mutton (though there are infinite variations), spiced with a piquant curry powder, vinegar, and apricot jam, topped with an egg custard. The flavor and texture are incredible—sweet and spicy, rich, with beautiful creaminess. This dish immediately became part of my own culinary arsenal.

The lesson extended beyond food, as I saw snippets of South Africa's complex history through her eyes—hearing about her family and upbringing, how she met her husband, and raising their children in the apartheid and post-apartheid eras. That night defined my trip. Culture, cuisine, and history wrapped up into one lasting memory.

South African Shepherd's Pie (Bobotie)

When it comes to homey, tasty comfort food, it doesn't get better than this. Bobotie is a South African classic similar to shepherd's pie—a casserole layered with sweet and spicy ground meat topped with an egg custard in lieu of the Western mashed potatoes. I like to use a meatball combo of beef, pork, and veal (⅓ of each), my own spice blend, and red currant jelly for a rich flavor. Oh, and making these in individual ramekins makes it easier to bake them off in a water bath, which gives a creamy, custardy texture to the egg topping (instead of a quiche-like one).

YIELDS 4 (10-OUNCE) RAMEKINS

For the meat filling:

1 slice white bread or brioche

⅔ cup milk

2–3 tablespoons canola oil

1 large yellow onion, finely chopped

1–2 green chilies (jalapeño or serrano)

¼ teaspoon minced ginger

3–4 garlic cloves, minced

½ teaspoon turmeric

½ teaspoon ground cumin

½ teaspoon ground coriander

¼ teaspoon ground garam masala

½ teaspoon hot Hungarian paprika

¼ teaspoon cayenne pepper

½ teaspoon ground black pepper

1¼ pounds ground meatball blend (⅓ each of beef/pork/veal)

4 tablespoons red currant or apricot preserves

2 tablespoons malt vinegar
1 plum tomato, roughly chopped
salt, to taste

For the egg custard:
4 eggs, beaten
¾ cup heavy cream
pinch salt
chives, sliced, for garnish

1. Preheat oven to 350°F.

2. Place bread in a bowl and cover with milk. Let sit until ready to use, turning if necessary to make sure the entire piece of bread is soaked.

3. Heat a large skillet over medium heat. Add oil and then the onions, chilies, and ginger with a bit of salt to draw out the moisture. Sauté for 4 to 5 minutes, until the onions are translucent. Add in the garlic and spices and sauté for another 30 seconds to a minute, until the garlic is fragrant.

4. Increase the heat to medium-high and push the vegetables aside a bit. Add the ground meat and brown for 3 to 4 minutes —you want to develop color and deepen the flavor of the ground meat. Using a wooden spoon or a spatula, break up the meat with the onions and spices to mix. Add the preserves, malt vinegar, and tomato and season with salt. Lower heat and simmer uncovered for 15 to 20 minutes for all of the flavors to meld. Taste and adjust seasoning.

5. Transfer mixture to a bowl using a slotted spoon and let cool briefly. Wring out excess milk from the bread and add to the meat mixture. Mix thoroughly. Fill 4 (10-ounce) ramekins ¾ full with meat mixture and place ramekins in a roasting pan or baking dish.

6. Combine eggs, heavy cream, and pinch of salt and pour to fill ramekins to the top. You want to bake these in a water bath, so fill the roasting pan or baking dish with boiling water until it comes at least halfway up the sides of the ramekins (see sidebar).

7. Cook at 350°F for 25 to 30 minutes or until the custard is set. You want the custard to be supple, so don't overcook or it turns into an omelet topping. If it jiggles a bit in the center, that's fine. Just let it sit in the water bath once you've taken it out of the oven to firm up a bit.

8. Let cool for a few minutes before serving. Serve in the ramekins topped with chopped chives.

A water bath is simply a pan of hot water in which you bake something like a custard or a cheesecake. The water insulates the dish from the direct heat of the oven and provides moisture circulation so your custard doesn't dry out. I like to start with a roasting pan and line it with paper towels. Then, I place the ramekins or other pan inside the roasting pan and (carefully!) fill halfway up with hot water. The paper towels prevent the ramekins from sliding, and filling up halfway means there's enough water so that it won't evaporate before the dish is done cooking.

Rosy's Beef and Potato Patties

These delicious patties are something my grandmother used to make for my dad growing up. The beef filling is simple, spiced with cumin and coriander, and tastes amazing on its own. The potato layer is pillowy and soft, a texture that works beautifully against that outer crust. Make a double batch and freeze these up for a quick lunch or dinner—they taste amazing with a dollop of spicy ketchup.

YIELDS 10–12 PATTIES

For the filling:

2–3 tablespoons canola oil

1 pound ground beef

1 teaspoon ground cumin

¾ teaspoon ground coriander

½ teaspoon chili powder

½ teaspoon ground garam masala

4–5 garlic cloves, minced

½ teaspoon minced ginger

1–2 green chilies (Thai or serrano), minced

1 medium yellow onion, finely chopped

salt and freshly ground black pepper, to taste

½ teaspoon fresh mint, finely chopped

1½ tablespoons fresh cilantro, finely chopped

For the potato:

3½ pounds Yukon gold potatoes, peeled and cut into a medium dice

salt and freshly ground black pepper, to taste

3 tablespoons unsalted butter, melted

1 squeeze lemon juice

2 teaspoons fresh cilantro, finely chopped

For the breading:

¼ cup flour

2 eggs, beaten

½ cup bread crumbs

canola oil, for frying

1. Heat a large sauté pan over high heat. Add the oil and the ground beef and sear for about 3 minutes. You want to brown up the meat. Break it up with a wooden spoon and sauté for another 2 minutes. Reduce the heat to medium and add the ground spices, garlic, ginger, chilies, and onion, and season generously with salt and freshly ground black pepper. The liquid from the beef and the vegetables should release a bit—you want this to simmer uncovered for 10 to 15 minutes. Remove to a separate bowl using a slotted spoon, mix in the fresh herbs, adjust seasoning to taste, and set aside.

2. Add diced potatoes and water to cover them to a medium pot. Bring up to a boil, season generously, and boil until potatoes are fork tender. Strain the potatoes and then pass them through a ricer or use a potato masher to mash them. Add the butter, lemon juice, and cilantro, and then season generously to taste.

3. Now, form the patties. Start with a ¼-cup dry measuring cup and scoop out measured amounts of the potato onto a parchment-lined baking sheet until all of the potato is finished. Then, take one (¼-cup) round of potato and flatten it with your palm. Add about 2 to 3 tablespoons of the ground beef mixture and top with another (¼-cup) round of the potato. Carefully seal the edges and mold with your hands to form a patty. The potato will be very soft, so you should work it gently. Continue until all of the potato and beef mixture is used up.

4. Set up a breading station with the flour, beaten eggs, and bread crumbs in separate bowls. Dip each patty first in the flour, shaking off the excess, then in the egg, and finally in the bread crumbs. Repeat until all are breaded.

5. Heat a large sauté pan with high sides over medium-high heat. Add oil until it reaches about 1" deep so you can shallow-fry the patties. When the oil is hot, carefully add the patties and fry for about 2 minutes per side, just to brown them. Work in batches if the pan isn't big enough.

6. Serve hot with a side of spicy ketchup.

Goat Biryani

Biryani is a celebratory dish: rice layered with chicken, beef, mutton, goat, vegetables, or seafood; aromatic with a serious spice blend; and topped with toasted nuts, dried fruit, and saffron milk. It's eaten throughout South Asia, brought in by the Persians, but different versions can also be found in South Africa, Thailand, Indonesia, and Iran (to name a few places). It's a process to be sure, but it's the time and love that makes this dish so beautiful. I used goat here, but feel free to try it with braising cuts of lamb or beef if that's more readily available.

SERVES 8–10

For the spice blend:
4 whole black peppercorns
4 whole cloves
2 cinnamon sticks
3 whole black cardamom pods, cracked open
1 teaspoon white cumin seeds
½ teaspoon aniseed
1 teaspoon nigella seeds (optional)
1 teaspoon dill seeds (optional)
2 crushed, dried bay leaves
1 pinch saffron
1 teaspoon turmeric
1½ teaspoons chili powder
¾ teaspoon ground fenugreek
1 teaspoon ground cumin
¾ teaspoon ground coriander
½ teaspoon sweet paprika

For the goat braise:

3½ pounds goat shoulder or leg, bone-in and cubed (see sidebar)

salt and freshly ground black pepper, to taste

3 tablespoons canola oil

2 medium white onions, thinly sliced

1 or 2 green chilies (Thai or serrano), finely chopped

10 garlic cloves, minced

2 teaspoons minced ginger

2 plum tomatoes, chopped

1 cup chicken, beef, or lamb stock

⅓ cup yogurt, beaten (beating yogurt with a whisk before adding it to a curry or stew will prevent the yogurt from "breaking," or separating)

8–10 mint leaves, chopped

large handful of cilantro, chopped

freshly squeezed lemon juice, to taste

For the rice:

3½ cups of basmati rice, rinsed until the water runs clear and drained

1 whole clove

2 whole black peppercorns

1 cinnamon stick

1 whole black cardamom pod, cracked open

salt, to taste

For the garnish:

¾ cup milk

pinch saffron

¼ cup sliced almonds, toasted

¼ cup cashews, toasted

¼ cup sultanas or golden raisins

1. Preheat oven to 350°F. Combine all the spice blend ingredients together and set aside.

2. Heat a Dutch oven or other heavy-bottomed pot that has a fitted lid over medium-high heat. Season the goat generously with salt and pepper. Add the oil and sear the meat for 2 minutes per side in batches to avoid overcrowding the pot. You want to develop a nice brown and overcrowding will steam the meat. Remove to a plate and set aside.

3. Turn heat down very slightly and add the onions to the same pot. Brown the onions to develop the signature taste of biryani. Cooking time will vary for this, but it takes about 20 to 25 minutes, stirring frequently. Add more oil if you need to. If you want to speed up the process, you can separately deep-fry these onions, but I like the caramelized flavor that develops from slow-cooking them. Remove onions to a separate plate.

4. Reduce the heat to medium. Add the spice blend, chilies, garlic, and ginger and cook for 3 to 4 minutes, being careful not to burn the spices. Reduce the heat as needed. You are looking for a change in the smell, a toasted nuttiness that will signify the spices are cooked.

5. Add back in the meat (along with any juices), ⅔ of the onions (reserving the other ⅓ for later), as well as the tomato and stock. Bring mixture up to a boil, cover, and place in the oven. Cook for 2 hours, stirring the pot at half-hour intervals. Remove from the oven, stir in the beaten yogurt, and place back in the oven for another 30 minutes, partially covered.

6. While the goat is cooking, work on the rice. Bring the rice, whole spices, and 5¼ cups water to a boil. Season generously with salt. Reduce to a simmer and simmer partially covered for 15 minutes. The rice will be partially cooked, which is what you want. Remove from the heat.

7. In the meantime, heat the milk in a small saucepan over medium heat until simmering. Add the saffron and turn off the heat. The saffron should infuse the liquid with its flavor and color (we are going to pour this over the rice at the end).

8. Remove the goat braise from the oven and add in the chopped mint and cilantro (reserving a few tablespoons for garnish). Add some lemon juice and season to taste.

9. You can either use another casserole dish to layer the biryani or you can transfer the goat to another bowl and use the same pot in which you cooked it. The bottom layer should be half of the goat braise. Top that with half of the rice and then repeat to finish the goat and the rice. Cover the top with the remaining browned onions, the toasted nuts, the golden raisins, and chopped herbs. Poke holes in the rice and pour the saffron-milk mixture all over the top. Cover tightly and place back in the oven for another 30 to 40 minutes, until the rice is cooked through.

10. Serve hot and with much fanfare for all the work you put in!

Although not so popular in the Western world, goat is eaten all over. If you aren't big on the gaminess and are cooking it for the first time, use the leg rather than the shoulder. I find a lot of that flavor resides in the fat, and the leg is much leaner than the shoulder.

Greek Lasagna

If you like lasagna, you will love this Greek-inspired version. Patsitsio is a Mediterranean baked pasta dish that layers meat sauce with pasta and béchamel. The meat sauce is surprisingly simple but packs a lot of flavor with a bit of cinnamon, bay leaves, and oregano. This is a serious meal and great to serve a big crowd—but the leftovers are even better. To make ahead of time, assemble and keep in the fridge until ready to bake.

SERVES 6–8

For the meat sauce:
3 tablespoons olive oil, plus extra for the pasta
1¼ pounds ground beef or meatball blend
2 medium yellow onions, roughly chopped
3 garlic cloves, minced
¼ cup white wine
2 cups canned crushed tomatoes
pinch chili flakes
2 fresh or dried bay leaves
1 teaspoon dried oregano
1 cinnamon stick

For the béchamel and pasta:
1 pound No. 2 Greek macaroni, bucatini, or rigatoni
3 eggs, separated
¾ cup grated Parmesan cheese, divided
6 tablespoons unsalted butter
¼ cup plus 2 tablespoons all-purpose flour
3 cups milk
salt and freshly ground black pepper, to taste
freshly grated nutmeg, to taste

1. Preheat the oven to 350°F.

2. For the meat sauce, heat a large pan with straight sides over medium-high heat. When hot, add the olive oil and then the ground beef and let sit for 2 to 3 minutes to develop a nice brown on the meat. Stir and cook for another 2 to 3 minutes at this heat and then reduce to medium. Add the onions and sauté for another 3 to 5 minutes until they are translucent. Add the minced garlic and let cook for 30 seconds to a minute, until it's fragrant.

3. Add the wine, crushed tomatoes, chili flakes, bay leaves, oregano, and cinnamon and simmer uncovered for 20 to 25 minutes. Remove the bay leaves and cinnamon stick and adjust the seasoning. Set aside until ready to assemble.

4. For the pasta, heat a large pot full of water over high heat. When it comes to a boil, season generously with salt to the point the cooking water tastes salty. Add the pasta and cook just a minute short of the package's recommended cook time. You want the pasta al dente because it will finish cooking in the oven. Drain and toss with olive oil. Lightly beat the 3 egg whites and add to the drained pasta along with ¼ cup of the grated Parmesan cheese. Mix to combine thoroughly.

5. In a medium pot, melt butter over medium heat and add flour. Whisk until the flour is fully incorporated and continue to cook out any raw flour taste for 2 to 3 minutes. Add milk and increase the heat to bring up to boil, whisking continuously to prevent lumps. Mixture should start to thicken and bubble. Lightly beat the 3 egg yolks in a bowl and add a few ladlefuls of the béchamel to bring the yolks up to temperature. Slowly add them back into the béchamel sauce and turn off the heat. Lastly, whisk in the remaining ½ cup grated Parmesan cheese and adjust the seasoning of the béchamel.

6. Now, you want to assemble the lasagna. Grease a 3-quart baking dish and add ⅔ of the pasta. Top with all the meat sauce and then the remaining ⅓ of the pasta. For the final layer, add all the béchamel.

7. Bake for 35 to 45 minutes until the béchamel is set and starting to brown. I like to throw it under the broiler for 2 to 3 minutes before serving to develop more brown on top, but watch because it browns quickly!

8. Let cool a bit before cutting—that way, it keeps its shape. Serve warm.

Chapter 7

VEGETABLES AND
SIDE DISHES

As I've gotten older, become more educated on farming traditions in the United States, and matched my cooking with the seasons, I love to enjoy the richness and full flavor peak-season vegetables have to offer.

Summer corn is one of my favorites, and I give a spiced-up version of the Southern classic corn pudding and an East African–inspired green chili and coriander version, roasted in the husks and all. Sautéed beet greens get a kick from garlic, chili, and fish sauce, and sweet potatoes mellow out in a pie crust with some chai spices.

There are a few other creative twists here as well, like a quinoa risotto, a "quinotto," studded with rich, fall wild mushrooms that I learned about during my travels. You'll also find a take on your traditional crumble dessert, a savory vegetable crumble with winter farmers' market offerings like squash, parsnips, and salsify. Play and work with the best, local, in-season ingredients to maximize flavor.

Corn with Green Chili Butter and Toasted Coconut

I grew up eating this rich corn curry—pieces of corn on the cob simmered in a delicious stew with coconut, green chilies, and cilantro. When summer comes around and corn is in season, I'm not usually in the mood for stews, so I came up with this recipe to satisfy my cravings—buttery, grilled corn with sweetness, heat, and the crunch of toasted coconut. VEGETARIAN, GLUTEN-FREE

SERVES 4–6

6 ears of corn

1 stick unsalted butter, room temperature

½ teaspoon salt

½ teaspoon honey

1 serrano chili, finely minced, seeds and ribs removed

2 tablespoons chopped cilantro

3 tablespoons unsweetened dessicated coconut, toasted

salt, to finish

1. Preheat the oven to 400°F or preheat the grill. Roast/grill corn in the husks for 25 minutes. Remove the husks and any remaining silk.

2. In a small bowl, combine butter, salt, honey, serrano chili, and cilantro.

3. Liberally spread chili butter on corn and sprinkle with the toasted coconut. Finish with a bit of salt and serve.

Wild Mushroom Quinotto

When I was traveling in Peru, I came across this truly delicious (and healthy) version of risotto using quinoa in lieu of the traditional arborio or carnaroli rice. Being a huge risotto fan, I played around with this substitution using different seasonal vegetables, but I always tend to come back to this simple mushroom version. The flavor is nuttier with earthiness from the mushrooms, and it has more texture than your traditional risotto. With quinoa's nutritional value, I love that I don't feel guilty when I whip this up on a weeknight. VEGETARIAN

SERVES 4–6

4–5 cups vegetable or chicken stock

2–3 tablespoons olive oil

4 cups chopped mixed wild mushrooms

2 tablespoons unsalted butter, divided

2 medium shallots, finely chopped

3–4 garlic cloves, minced

2 cups raw quinoa

½ cup white wine

¼ cup heavy cream

½ cup grated Parmesan, Grana Padano, or other grated cheese

salt and freshly ground black pepper, to taste

chives or cilantro, to garnish

1. In a saucepan, bring the stock up to a boil and reduce to a simmer while you are working on the other ingredients.

2. Heat a large sauté pan with straight sides over high heat. Add the oil and when it starts to shimmer, add about half the mushrooms. You don't want to overcrowd the pan, and the mushrooms should be in a single layer. Leave them for 2 to 3 minutes to develop a nice golden brown. Add 1 tablespoon of butter, season with salt, and toss to cook another minute. Remove using a slotted spoon and repeat with the rest of the mushrooms and another tablespoon of butter. Set aside.

3. Reduce heat to medium-low and add shallots and garlic. Cook for 3 to 4 minutes, until translucent, and then add quinoa. Toast for about a minute and then add the white wine. Let it reduce by half and then stir in about 2 cups of the hot stock. Continue adding stock, a ½ cup at a time, stirring at intervals for 15 minutes. You'll need between 4 and 5 cups of stock to achieve a "risotto-like" texture. Cover for the last 5 minutes.

4. Add in the reserved mushrooms, heavy cream, cheese, and season to taste. Serve immediately, garnished with fresh herbs.

Roasted Cauliflower with Bread Crumbs, Saffron, and Dried Cranberries

I love roasting vegetables, particularly cauliflower, to bring out and caramelize their natural sweetness. I was inspired by a Sicilian cauliflower and pasta dish to upgrade my nightly roasted vegetable with the addition of saffron, capers, bread crumbs, and pine nuts. I used cranberries here in lieu of the traditional golden raisins or currants, and the result is a sweet, salty, and sour mix of flavors and textures. VEGETARIAN

SERVES 4

1 head of cauliflower, cut into florets

a few tablespoons of olive oil

salt and freshly ground black pepper, to taste

¼ cup chicken or vegetable stock

pinch saffron

¼ cup dried cranberries

1 tablespoon unsalted butter

1 garlic clove, minced

2 tablespoons capers, rinsed and drained

¼ cup bread crumbs

¼ cup pine nuts, toasted

small handful of flat leaf parsley, finely chopped

1. Preheat the oven to 400°F.

2. In a large bowl, toss the cauliflower together with a bit of olive oil, salt, and pepper. Spread out on a baking sheet into a single layer. Roast for 25 to 30 minutes, until brown at the tips.

3. In the meantime, in a small saucepan, bring the stock up to a boil, add the saffron and cranberries, and remove from the heat.

4. In a small sauté pan, melt the butter over medium heat. When the foam starts to subside, add the garlic and sauté 30 seconds to a minute, until fragrant. Add the capers for another 30 seconds and then the bread crumbs. Toast for a minute or two, until golden brown, and then remove from the heat.

5. Toss the cauliflower together with the saffron/cranberry mixture and the toasted pine nuts. Top with the capers and bread crumbs and some chopped parsley and serve immediately.

The technique used here works well on other vegetables—from broccoli to Brussels sprouts to summer squash. Start with *dry* vegetables cut into uniform pieces, coated in oil, and well seasoned. Space them out on a baking sheet (or multiple) so there is room between the pieces. Roast in a hot oven—the time will vary depending on what size you cut the vegetables.

Patatas Bravas–Inspired Salad

Patatas bravas is classic Spanish tapas, crispy-fried potatoes topped with Catalan allioli. This was the inspiration for a potato salad with a bit more texture than the traditional kind. To make it a bit healthier, I opted to roast the potatoes to get them crispy before tossing them with the vegetables and aioli (Catalan allioli doesn't contain egg, so my "mayo" is technically a Provençal aioli). VEGETARIAN

SERVES 4–6

For the potato salad:

4 pounds small creamer potatoes, scrubbed and halved

2 teaspoons white vinegar

olive oil

salt and freshly ground black pepper

1 green onion, minced

1 small red onion or 2 shallots, minced

1 stalk of celery, minced

For the aioli:

1 egg yolk

½ teaspoon Dijon mustard

2½ teaspoons freshly squeezed lemon juice

5 garlic cloves, minced

¾ teaspoon smoked Spanish paprika (optional)

pinch salt

½ cup olive oil

1. Preheat oven to 500°F.

2. *For the potato salad:* In a medium pot, cover potatoes with cold water by 2". Add vinegar and season generously with salt. Bring up to a boil and boil for 5 minutes. Drain and let dry a few minutes.

3. Transfer potatoes to a large bowl and drizzle with olive oil. Season generously with salt and pepper. Divide potatoes between two baking sheets and bake for 30 to 35 minutes, flipping the potatoes midway through.

4. *For the aioli:* In a bowl, whisk together the egg yolk with the Dijon mustard, lemon juice, minced garlic, smoked Spanish paprika (if using), and salt. Slowly drizzle in the olive oil, whisking continuously until the mixture emulsifies.

5. In a large bowl, toss the potatoes together with the green onion, red onion, celery, and aioli.

6. Serve warm and immediately.

Importance of Ingredients

When you grow up with multicultural cuisine, sourcing the proper ingredients becomes incredibly important. For my family, it was never a one-stop shop at the grocery store to pick everything up; no one grocery store ever had everything we needed. So it was on to the Middle Eastern store for the best rice; then the Indian store for spices, hard-to-find ingredients, and the finest-tasting cilantro. Then, we'd head to the Latin market for cassava and the most aromatic mangoes for breakfast. It really became second nature to me that I would always "boutique" shop for my ingredients.

Flash forward to my work in the professional kitchens, and it's no different. We source from many different purveyors, obviously comparing price, but also to achieve the highest quality mix of products. When specific produce is in season or certain fish are readily available and the prices drop, the focus is always on food costs and producing the dishes that best work within our budgets, with the benefit that peak season means peak flavor.

Traveling to different countries, I watch and chat with locals at the markets who shop almost on a daily basis. In many places, fruit comes to the market ripe and is bought and consumed immediately. Many people like to eat fresh food, and they buy that day what they plan to cook. There's a connectivity there, an inherent knowledge of the seasons and what to look for, and their diet ebbs and flows with the rhythms of the year.

Living in New York City, I am extremely fortunate to have access to a lot of different types of ingredients and thriving farmers' markets. But if you live in a spot where grocery stores don't adequately reflect or tell the story of exactly from where and how those ingredients came to you, check in with local chefs and see where they source their ingredients.

Throughout this book, but particularly as you look at the vegetables in this section, it's important to work with what's in season and think about food sourcing. If you can, get out to local farms or make the farmers' market a regular stop. You will taste the difference for yourself, and those who eat your cooking will thank you for it.

Savory Winter Vegetable Crumble

Although I love fruit crumbles, this savory crumble is a close second. I tend to go a bit wild at the farmers' market, and this dish is a great way to use up scraps of winter vegetables you might have lying around. It's all about great textural balance: the salty, Parmy topping adds the perfect crunch to the sweet and tender vegetables flecked with those crunchy bits of nuts and tart currants. It's a dish that takes 5 minutes to prep and works in the oven, freeing you to work on the rest of the meal. VEGETARIAN

SERVES 6–8 (YIELDS 1 [2-QUART] BAKING DISH)

For the crumble:

¼ cup flour

2 tablespoons bread crumbs

2 tablespoons cold, unsalted butter, cut into small cubes

1 tablespoon Parmesan cheese

¼ teaspoon salt

pinch ground black pepper

For the vegetables:

7 cups mixed vegetables, cut into a ½" dice (butternut squash, sunchokes, sweet potatoes, salsify, parsnips, or even romanesco cauliflower)

1 shallot, minced

2–3 garlic cloves, minced

2–3 tablespoons dried currants or pitted dried cherries

3 tablespoons pine nuts or crushed almonds

salt and freshly ground black pepper, to taste

olive oil, to coat

1. Preheat the oven to 375°F.

2. *For the crumble:* To the bowl of a food processor, add all of the crumble ingredients and pulse until it forms a coarse meal. Set aside.

3. *For the vegetables:* In a large bowl, combine the mixed vegetables with the minced shallot, garlic, dried currants, and nuts. Season with salt and pepper and drizzle with olive oil. Toss to coat evenly.

4. Transfer the vegetables to a 2-quart baking dish and smooth out the top. Sprinkle the crumble on top and bake for an hour.

5. Serve hot and immediately.

Smoky Corn Pudding with Mustard Seeds and Curry Leaves

Growing up in Florida (yes, it's still the South!), I developed such a weakness for Southern food. Corn pudding is classic, Southern comfort food at its best. There are tons of variations and no real "right" way to make corn pudding, but I prefer this method because it stays creamy and sweet, with a caramelized top, and it still cuts easily without being bread-like. I use the combo of mustard seeds and curry leaves, and this marries incredibly well with the sweetness of the corn, the spiciness from the peppers, the tang of the sun-dried tomatoes, and the deep, lovely smokiness from the mozzarella. This dish is simply divine. VEGETARIAN

SERVES 6–8 (YIELDS 1 [2-QUART] BAKING DISH)

To roast the corn:
4–6 medium ears of corn, husks and silk removed (you want about 3½ cups of the kernels)
olive oil, for brushing
salt and freshly ground black pepper, to taste

For the corn pudding:
1 tablespoon olive oil
2 tablespoons unsalted butter
1½ tablespoons black or brown mustard seeds
10 curry leaves
2 shallots, finely chopped
1 red cherry, Fresno, or jalapeño pepper, minced
3 garlic cloves, minced
1 tablespoon finely chopped sundried tomatoes (either packed in oil or rehydrated)
¼ cup all-purpose flour

3 whole eggs

2 cups heavy cream

a couple of dashes of Tabasco

1¼ teaspoons salt

½ teaspoon ground black pepper

1¼ cups grated smoked mozzarella

¼ cup sliced green onions, dark and light green parts only

1. The first step of this dish is roasting or grilling the corn. Brush the corn with olive oil and season with salt and pepper. Place cobs on a hot grill and cook for 20 minutes, rotating every few minutes to cook all sides. If you don't have a grill, you can place the seasoned corn on a baking sheet under the broiler for the same amount of time (still rotating). Let cool slightly, cut the kernels from the cobs, and reserve kernels in a separate bowl.

2. Preheat the oven to 350°F.

3. In a medium skillet, heat the olive oil and butter on medium-high heat. Once foam subsides, add the mustard seeds and curry leaves. Once the seeds start to sputter and pop after 30 seconds to 1 minute, lower the heat to medium-low and add shallots, peppers, and a pinch of salt. Cook for a few minutes, until shallots are translucent. Add garlic and cook 30 seconds, until fragrant. Add sundried tomatoes, corn kernels, and flour and stir to coat. Cook for another 30 seconds, stirring. Remove from heat and transfer to a large bowl.

4. In a separate bowl, beat together eggs, cream, Tabasco, salt, and pepper. Add this along with the grated smoked mozzarella and the green onions to the corn mixture and combine thoroughly. Transfer to a greased 2-quart baking dish and bake for 50 minutes or until an inserted knife comes out clean.

5. Let cool slightly before serving.

Garlicky Beet Greens with Fish Sauce and Chili

If you are like me, you hate wasting. I save scraps of onions, lemon halves, chopped herbs, chicken bones, duck fat, spice blends, etc., until my fridge and kitchen look ridiculous. Beets are delicious, but I can never throw away the super healthy greens that top them. In fact, they stand on their own and make a gorgeous sauté so there is no reason to get rid of them. Here, with some garlic, fish sauce, rice vinegar, and chili, they are transformed into an incredibly flavorful side dish. Enjoy these with your roasted beets and a simple protein.

SERVES 4

3 bunches beet greens, thoroughly washed (see sidebar)

3 tablespoons olive oil

1 shallot, minced

3–4 garlic cloves, minced

2¼ teaspoons fish sauce

¾ teaspoon honey

¾ teaspoon rice vinegar

¼ to ½ teaspoon chili sauce (like sriracha)

salt and freshly ground black pepper, to taste

1. Make sure the beet greens are dry and trim off any thick stems. I take them down to within 1" or 2" of where the leaves start.

2. Heat a very large saucepan over medium heat. You want a large surface area, so the liquid will evaporate quickly and you won't have watery greens. When it's hot, add the oil, shallot, and garlic along with a bit of salt to draw out the moisture. Sauté for a minute or two, until the shallots are translucent.

3. Pile the beet greens on top and let them wilt for 2 minutes. While they are wilting, whisk together the fish sauce, honey, rice vinegar, and chili sauce. Pour this on top and then use tongs to rotate the greens so the raw portions get to cook down. Cook for another minute or two, until all of the greens are just wilted but still have a deep color. Taste and adjust seasoning.

4. Serve immediately.

Triple-washing greens is an important step we use in restaurants to make sure they are clean. Beet greens are notoriously sandy and gritty, so start with two large bowls. Add the greens to one bowl, fill with cold water and swoosh them around to loosen the dirt. Lift them out carefully and put them in the other bowl, fill with water, and repeat. Wash the first bowl before transferring the greens back in for the third wash because all of the sand and grit sinks to the bottom. After three washes, the greens should be clean!

Don't Let the Pepper Burst!

When I went to culinary school, it was to learn basic French technique—an important building block in Western cooking. But each time I've worked at an ethnic restaurant or visited a new country and had the locals teach me, I walk away learning a slew of new dishes, which ingredients are core to their cooking, and almost always nuggets of wisdom on their culture-specific techniques, which I love to apply to other dishes.

When my husband's aunt from Trinidad, Aunt Cherry, came up one Thanksgiving, we spent a week together, and she taught me all the dishes she could (I had her on a bit of a grueling schedule). We hunted around the West Indian markets deep in Brooklyn to get all her favorite ingredients, and she taught me stewed goat and chicken, curried chicken, how to make callaloo, sweet bread, cassava pone, and macaroni pie, to name a few . . . .

One of my favorite dishes she taught me was *peas and rice*, a dish that was passed on from her mother. We burned the sugar, added the salt pork, and cooked down the onions, garlic, and green onions in the sweetened fat. Then, we threw in a bit of *chandon beni* (culantro, an herb that tastes like cilantro) with the pigeon peas, some stock, coconut milk, and parboiled rice.

The last step, and this is important, was adding in the pepper. Now, this is not just any pepper . . . it's a Scotch bonnet pepper, which if you've ever tried is like having a five-alarm fire go off in your mouth. The thing about Scotch bonnet peppers is that, if you could take away some of the heat, the flavor is gorgeous! The genius part of the peas and rice recipe? You throw the pepper into the rice whole and take it out before it bursts, getting *all* the flavor of that killer chili and just a tiny bit of that killer heat. Genius, I say.

I've since used this technique in other rice dishes, soups, and stews—I love the idea of the flavor infusion of the pepper and minimizing the scorch-inducing effects. Contrary to the rule, I have, indeed (accidentally), let the pepper burst, and my guests politely guzzled water with their rice that time. Oops! But this little nugget is definitely key in my cooking arsenal. Thank you again, Aunt Cherry!

Gran's Peas and Rice

West Indian peas and rice is a dish I crave regularly—rice cooked with coconut milk, pigeon peas, smoky and sweet from the browning with a touch of heat from a Scotch bonnet pepper. This is pure comfort and great as an accompaniment to everything from barbecue to grilled fish to stews. This dish definitely steps up your rice game. GLUTEN-FREE

SERVES 6–8

2–4 tablespoons canola oil

3 tablespoons light brown or palm sugar

¼ pound salt pork, 1 thick-cut strip of bacon, or 1 to 2 good bones (see sidebar)

2 medium yellow onions, finely chopped

1 green onion, finely chopped

½ teaspoon minced ginger

4–5 garlic cloves, minced

2 cups parboiled long-grain rice*

2 (15-ounce) cans pigeon peas, drained and rinsed thoroughly

1 (13½-ounce) can coconut milk

2 cups chicken or vegetable stock

1 Scotch bonnet or habanero chili pepper

1 fresh or dried bay leaf

1 small bunch of thyme, tied together

2 tablespoons finely chopped cilantro, plus more for garnish

salt and freshly ground black pepper, to taste

1. Preheat the oven to 350°F.

2. Heat a large pot or Dutch oven over medium heat. Add the oil and when it starts to shimmer, add the sugar and cook until the sugar liquefies and the oil just starts to smoke (see instructions in *How to Make Browning*). Throw in the salt pork, onions, ginger, garlic, and a bit of salt and reduce the heat to medium-low. Sauté for 5 to 7 minutes, until the onions are translucent.

3. Now, add in the rice, pigeon peas, coconut milk, stock, the whole, uncut pepper, the bay leaf, thyme, and the 2 tablespoons of cilantro. Season generously with salt and freshly ground black pepper at this point. Bring up to a boil and then place in the oven, covered, for 20 minutes.

4. Switch the oven off after 20 minutes and partially remove the cover but leave it in the hot oven for another 5 to 10 minutes. This will help dry out the rice a bit.

5. Remove the pepper. (It shouldn't have popped! If it did, you might be in for it . . . .) Remove the bay leaf and thyme bunch and add in a small handful of chopped cilantro to garnish. You can also season again at this point but be careful not to break up the rice too much. Serve hot!

*Parboiled rice is rice that has been partially boiled in the husk before being polished, and I actually used parboiled basmati rice here. This process helps the rice retain a higher level of nutrition (similar to brown rice), cook faster, and stay separate and less sticky. You can easily use traditional, long-grain rice here; I'd just suggest rinsing off the starches thoroughly before cooking and adjusting your cook time based on which type of rice you choose.

Traditionally, a chunk or two of salt pork is used to create a base level of flavor for this rice dish, but I've used bacon, a gorgeous marrow bone, and even a leftover short rib (already cooked!) in the past. Obviously, if you are making a vegetarian version, you can leave this step out and still get tasty results.

Summer Squash and Burst Cherry Tomatoes with Brown Butter, Coriander, and Hazelnuts

The farmers' market in the summer is a continual draw, and I always find myself with tons of surplus. Sweet summer squash and juicy cherry tomatoes pair beautifully here and roast up in no time. I add a touch of brown butter and coriander for depth of flavor and nuttiness, and the hazelnuts fit right in and add great crunch. This is easy summer cooking at its finest. VEGETARIAN, GLUTEN-FREE

SERVES 6–8

2½ pounds mixed summer squash, cut into a medium dice
(approximately 3 squash and 3 zucchini)

1 pint cherry tomatoes, whole (approximately ¾ pound)

olive oil, to coat

salt and freshly ground black pepper, to taste

4 tablespoons unsalted butter

1 teaspoon ground coriander

½ cup hazelnuts, toasted

1. Preheat oven to 400°F.

2. In a large bowl, toss together the summer squash and tomatoes with olive oil to coat and some salt and freshly ground black pepper. Spread out over 1 large or 2 medium baking sheets. You want space between the vegetables so that they roast and don't steam. Roast for 15 to 20 minutes, until the tomatoes have burst and the squash are tender with a bit of firmness.

3. In a small saucepan, heat the butter with the coriander over medium heat. Swirl the pan from time to time as the butter melts. You want to watch for when the foam subsides, the milk solids deepen and turn brown, and the butter starts to smell nutty. (This is making brown butter.) As soon as you see these changes, transfer to another bowl—butter goes from brown to burnt quickly.

4. Toss the cooked squash and tomatoes with the browned, coriander butter and the toasted hazelnuts. Adjust seasoning and serve immediately.

Browning butter is a process where the milk solids in the butter are cooked until they are toasted, take on a golden brown color, and develop a deep nutty aroma. Use brown butter to add depth to dishes or even in place of melted butter in baking!

Chai-Spiced Sweet Potato Pie

I came up with this recipe to round out my holiday table. Sweet potato pie is a Southern classic, and chai spices work beautifully with the sweetness of the filling. This is my fool-proof pie crust, but feel free to use store-bought if you are pressed for time. VEGETARIAN

YIELDS 1 (9") PIE

For the crust:

1½ cups all-purpose flour

½ teaspoon salt

2 teaspoons sugar

1 stick cold, unsalted butter, cut into small cubes

2 tablespoons vegetable shortening, chilled and cut into small pieces

4–4½ tablespoons ice water

1 egg, beaten with a bit of heavy cream

For the filling:

8 tablespoons unsalted butter

½ cup evaporated milk

¾ cup brown sugar

1 teaspoon salt

2 cups roughly mashed, cooked sweet potatoes

3 egg yolks

1 teaspoon vanilla extract

For the chai spices:
½ teaspoon ground cinnamon
½ teaspoon ground cardamom
¼ teaspoon ground nutmeg
⅛ teaspoon ground clove
¼ teaspoon ground ginger
⅛ teaspoon ground black pepper

1. Preheat the oven to 375°F.

2. *For the crust*: In a food processor, pulse together the flour, salt, and sugar. Distribute the cold butter cubes and shortening over the flour and pulse until the mixture resembles a coarse meal. Pulse in the water, 1 tablespoon at a time, until the dough comes together in the bowl of the processor. It will start to clump up, but you don't want it to get too moist.

3. Turn the dough out onto plastic wrap and gently push together with your hands to form a flat disk. Wrap in plastic and refrigerate for at least an hour.

4. *For the filling*: Melt the butter with the evaporated milk over medium heat. Add the brown sugar and salt and whisk to dissolve. Transfer to the bowl of a food processor along with the cooked sweet potatoes, egg yolks, vanilla extract, and chai spices. Process until the mixture is smooth and all of the ingredients are evenly distributed.

5. On a floured surface or between parchment paper, roll out the dough to a 12" diameter circle and place carefully in a 9" pie dish. Trim the edges of excess and crimp the edges. Dock the dough lightly with a fork and place a piece of parchment paper on top. Add dried beans to weigh down the dough and blind bake for 15 minutes.

6. Reduce the temperature to 350°F. Remove the dried beans and parchment and fill with the sweet potato mixture. Brush the edges of the crust with the egg wash (egg beaten with heavy cream). Bake for 45 minutes, until the sweet potato is set.

7. Let cool completely at room temperature before cutting.

Cassava Fries with Chili-Lime Salt

From my Dad's East African side, I grew up eating cassava in many different ways—boiled with salt and red chili, stewed in rich spices and coconut milk, and (my favorite way) fried. Fried "mogo" is a delicious substitute for fries—they are light and crunchy, and the chili-lime salt adds just the right kick here. Enjoy! VEGAN, GLUTEN-FREE

SERVES 4–6

coconut oil or any fry oil

4 cassava roots, peeled and cut into ½" thick sticks

1 teaspoon salt

¼ teaspoon lime zest

pinch chili powder

squeeze of lime juice

1. Heat 2" to 3" of oil in a large saucepot or Dutch oven to 400°F.

2. In the meantime, fill a large pot with cold water and add cut cassava. Bring up to a boil and boil uncovered for 3 minutes. Drain cassava and dry on a cooling rack. I like to pat them with paper towels as well.

3. Combine salt, lime zest, and chili powder in a small bowl and set aside.

4. Carefully drop cassava in the oil and cook until golden brown, about 2 minutes. Drain on a cooling rack and sprinkle with chili salt.

5. Serve immediately, finished with a bit of lime juice.

Chapter 8

BREAKFAST, SAVORY TARTS, AND BREADS

I had a lot of fun cooking the recipes in this section, mostly because Sunday is one of my favorite cooking days of the week, and these recipes are fantastic for lingering weekend brunches.

The name of the game here is sweet and savory—I tried to provide a mix of both because it's nice to have options. A Maghrebi baked egg and tomato dish called shakshouka gets a bit of salty texture and bite with the addition of chorizo and bread crumbs, and I think quiche for breakfast is perfectly acceptable, particularly when it's inspired by huevos rancheros. On the sweeter side of things, a simple and healthy seed that dates back to the Aztecs and Mayans is turned into a pudding and fruit parfait, and the Latin combo of guava and cheese is worked into a breakfast Danish.

I love each and every one of these dishes, and I hope you have as much fun eating them as you do cooking them!

Shakshouka with Chorizo and Bread Crumbs

The Maghreb region incorporates the northwest portion of Africa—Tunisia, Morocco, Libya, Algeria, and Mauritania. Shakshouka is a mainstay of the region—baked eggs over an onion and tomato sauce that's eaten for breakfast or supper—and has even made its way to Israel, where it's an extremely popular dish. The main ingredients for the dish are tomatoes, onions, garlic, and eggs, and it differs from country to country, city to city, family to family. It can be as simple or extravagant as you like—I tailored this version to my tastes, but feel free to make it your own!

SERVES 4–6

¾ teaspoon white cumin seeds

1 link of fresh chorizo, cut into a fine dice

4 tablespoons olive oil, divided

2 medium yellow onions, thinly sliced

3–4 red peppers, mix of hot and small sweet, or 1 red bell pepper, thinly sliced

pinch saffron

1 teaspoon smoked Spanish paprika

3 garlic cloves, thinly sliced

4 sprigs thyme

2 bay leaves, fresh or dried

2 pounds plum tomatoes, roughly chopped

3 tablespoons cilantro, chopped

salt and freshly ground black pepper, to taste

6 whole large eggs

3 tablespoons bread crumbs

thick-cut toast, for serving

1. Preheat the broiler and place the oven rack on the second rung from the top.

2. Heat a 13" cast-iron pan over medium heat. Add cumin seeds and dry toast until fragrant and a bit deeper in color. Add chorizo, bump the heat up a notch, and lightly brown for 2 to 3 minutes. Remove from pan with a slotted spoon and set aside. Add 3 tablespoons of olive oil, sliced onions, peppers, saffron, and paprika and cook for 6 to 8 minutes, until onions are translucent. Add garlic, thyme, and bay leaves and sauté another minute or two, until the garlic is fragrant. Add in the thyme stems whole, let the leaves fall off, and pull out the stems later. If you want to remove the leaves from the stems before adding, feel free.

3. Now, add in the roughly chopped tomatoes (seeds and all!) and cook for another 12 to 15 minutes, until the tomatoes have softened, much of the liquid has evaporated, and the dish has taken on a thick, sauce-like consistency.

4. Remove the thyme stems, if left in, and bay leaves. Add the chopped cilantro, reserving 1 tablespoon for garnish, add back in the chorizo, and adjust seasoning.

5. Carefully, crack the eggs over the sauce so that the eggs are distributed evenly across the surface. Sprinkle the tops of the eggs with a bit of salt. In a small bowl, toss together bread crumbs and the remaining tablespoon of olive oil. Sprinkle over tomato and egg mixture. Cover the dish with foil and place under the broiler for 5 to 6 minutes. Remove foil and place under broiler for another 2 to 3 minutes, until the bread crumbs are lightly toasted.

6. Garnish with remaining chopped cilantro and serve hot with thick-cut pieces of toast.

Mexican Breakfast Quiche

I'm a huge fan of huevos rancheros, but sometimes I can't go for such a heavy meal so early in the day. I tried to capture some of my favorite flavors from that dish here in a simple and delicious quiche. The crust is super flaky, buttery, and delicious (my go-to crust for savory tarts), and I always make a double batch of it and freeze the other portion to use another time. VEGETARIAN

YIELDS 1 (9") TART

For the crust:

1½ cups all-purpose flour

1 teaspoon salt

½ teaspoon sugar

1 stick cold, unsalted butter, cut into small cubes

1 egg

1–3 teaspoons water

For the filling:

¼ small white onion, minced

3 garlic cloves, minced

1½ tablespoons pickled jalapeño slices, minced (or regular jalapeño, seeded and minced)

½ plum tomato, seeded, juice removed, and finely chopped

¼ teaspoon lime zest

1 tablespoon chopped cilantro

½ cup shredded Cheddar or pepper jack cheese

4 large eggs

¾ cup heavy cream

1. *For the crust*: In a food processor, pulse together flour, salt, and sugar. Scatter the cold cubes of butter over the dry ingredients and pulse until the butter is cut in and the texture looks like sandy peas or a coarse meal. In a small bowl, lightly beat together the egg and 1 teaspoon of the water. Add in increments, pulsing, until the dough sticks together. If the dough still looks dry and doesn't hold together when pinched, pulse in another 1 to 2 teaspoons of water until it does. There will still be a lot of crumbly bits that haven't incorporated—that's okay.

2. Turn the dough out onto a work surface or a piece of parchment paper. LIGHTLY, knead the dough to make sure everything is incorporated. I literally just press it together a bit. Place into plastic wrap and create a flattened disk. Refrigerate for a minimum of 2 to 3 hours (and up to a day).

3. On a floured work surface or in between pieces of parchment paper (with flour), carefully roll out the dough with a rolling pin until uniform thickness and large enough for a 9" or 9½" tart shell. Carefully transfer to the *greased* tart shell and press carefully into the sides. Try not to stretch the dough at all. Trim any excess edges and dock (or prick holes all over) the surface of the dough with a fork. Wrap shell in plastic wrap and freeze for a minimum of a half hour.

4. Preheat the oven to 375°F. Remove tart shell from freezer and plastic wrap from tart and place on a baking sheet. Fit a piece of parchment paper on the surface of the dough and weigh it down with dried beans or baking weights. Bake on the middle rack for 20 minutes. Remove baking weights or beans and parchment paper and bake for another 10 minutes to brown. Let cool slightly.

5. Turn oven temperature down to 350°F and place the rack on the lowest level. Scatter the onion, garlic, jalapeño, tomato, lime zest, and cilantro evenly in the tart shell. Top with the cheese. Beat together the eggs and the heavy cream and pour into the tart shell to cover the ingredients. Bake for 25 minutes or until the custard is set.

6. Let cool slightly before cutting and serving.

Vanilla-Cinnamon
Chia Pudding Parfait

Chia seeds have worked their way into my morning ritual, and this is one of the many ways I enjoy them. They're a superfood, native to parts of Mexico and Guatemala, and are amazing in this "pudding parfait." The little seeds can hold 9 to 12 times their weight in liquid, so when added to water or milk here, they swell up, become gelatinous, and take on a pudding-like texture. With hints of vanilla and cinnamon and layered with fresh fruit and toasted nuts, this is a great way to start the day. VEGETARIAN, GLUTEN-FREE

YIELDS 4–6 SERVINGS

½ cup chia seeds

½ teaspoon ground cinnamon

2¼ cups regular, low-fat, or almond milk

1 teaspoon vanilla extract

1 tablespoon honey

½ cup sliced almonds, toasted

1½ cups mixed berries

1. In a medium bowl, add the chia and the cinnamon. Pour in the milk, whisking to make sure the chia doesn't clump and the cinnamon mixes in thoroughly.

2. Add the vanilla and honey and whisk to combine. Chill for a minimum of 30 minutes.

3. Layer the pudding over the nuts and berries and top with both. Serve chilled.

Chia acts as a complete protein, has more calcium than skim milk on a per-ounce basis, and is the richest plant source of omega-3.

Crab Kedgeree

Kedgeree is one of those migratory foods, an Anglo-Indian dish derived from khichdi, a popular South Asian dish of rice and lentils. The British version is often eaten for breakfast and typically features cooked, flaked smoked haddock, and although I put this in the breakfast section, you could easily catch me eating this for dinner. I also love using crab here because it saves a step since it's cooked already and adds that lovely sweet flavor. This hits your palate all over—heat, spice, sweetness, a touch of acidity from the lemon juice, and the sour creaminess of yogurt with it. Breakfast, lunch, or dinner . . . this is just a great one-pot meal. Enjoy! GLUTEN-FREE

SERVES 4–6

2 tablespoons canola oil

2 tablespoons unsalted butter, divided

1 tablespoon black or brown mustard seeds

½ teaspoon white cumin seeds

8–10 curry leaves (optional)

1 large yellow onion, finely chopped

1 jalapeño, finely chopped

½ teaspoon minced ginger

4 garlic cloves, minced

1 pound jumbo lump or lump crab, picked through for any shells

½ teaspoon turmeric

¼–½ teaspoon chili powder

1½ teaspoons ground coriander

¾ teaspoon ground cumin

1½ cups basmati rice, rinsed of starchy residue

1 dried bay leaf

3 cups chicken or vegetable stock or water

squeeze of lemon juice

handful of cilantro, chopped

salt and freshly ground black pepper, to taste

2 hard-boiled eggs, quartered

yogurt on the side

1. Heat a medium pot over medium-high heat. Add the oil and 1 tablespoon of the butter. Once the foam has subsided, add the mustard seeds, cumin seeds, and curry leaves if using. Stir and when they start to pop, throw in the onion, jalapeño, ginger, and a bit of salt to draw out the moisture and reduce the heat to medium. Sauté for 5 to 7 minutes, until the onions are translucent. Add the garlic, crab, turmeric, chili powder, coriander, and cumin and sauté for another 1 to 2 minutes.

2. Now, toss in the basmati rice, bay leaf, and stock or water and a few pinches of salt. Turn the heat up and bring up to a boil. Lower to a simmer and simmer partially covered for 20 to 25 minutes, until the rice is cooked through. Throw in the remaining tablespoon of butter, add a generous squeeze of lemon juice along with some fresh chopped cilantro and adjust seasoning to taste.

3. Serve immediately with 1 to 2 wedges of boiled egg and a dollop of yogurt on the side.

This is a fantastic "leftover" dish and, with cooked rice on hand, can be made in under 10 minutes. Once the crab and spices have sautéed a bit, throw in the cooked rice, brown up like a fried rice, and finish off with the lemon juice and cilantro.

The Beauty of
Sunday Cooking and Eating

Sunday in my house has always been a big cooking day. Growing up, my mom and I would work on a few dishes for a big midday brunch and then finish the day prepping for the week's cooking—washing and chopping vegetables, making lentils or other stews that can be eaten for days, and generally organizing ourselves.

This was my weekly culinary boot camp, where knife skills would get put to the test and I'd have to start distinguishing the spices in my mom's *dhaba* from sight and smell alone. A *dhaba*, by the way, is a spice box of sorts, a round metal container with smaller, round spice holders set inside. My mom's always held a sort of magic for me—she intuitively added a few pinches here and there with barely a glance, and I was jealous of how the dish always tasted amazingly consistent as if by alchemy.

It was on a Sunday that a visiting aunt taught me how to make my first East African dish, these savory puffs called *mandazis* (on the next page). Eating them was such a treat, reserved for family visits, and I was dying to know how to make them so I could eat them more often! Even then, I recognized how precious certain foods were—the secrets of their recipes held by a few key people. Of course, that made the dishes seem that much more special at the time, but as I grew older, it made me fear for the day that knowledge would disappear along with the generation.

Many people view dinner as the central meal, but for me Sunday brunch always anchored the week. Snacking on sweet and savory foods, with fresh fruit and tea, and adding dishes to the table as they became ready, this was a meal that would linger for hours, a time to catch up, download the week's happenings, a tradition of talk. It still is, to this day, a big deal—I hold weekend brunch as sacred and a time for my family, and I truly look forward to the day when I'll hold my own culinary boot camp.

East African Donuts (Mandazis)

These donuts are my childhood, one of those mysterious recipes only the old-school aunties and grandmas knew how to make. I begged an aunt to teach me, and even now, I feel I have to pass on the tradition! I should be clear: I'm calling them donuts but mandazis are actually savory. They shouldn't be too sweet or too salty. One of my most treasured food memories is sitting, facing the Indian Ocean, in Dar Es Salaam, Tanzania, using the (hollow) mandazis to scoop up a tender stew of pigeon peas in coconut milk with fresh chilies and cilantro (called barazi). But, of course, you can eat them however you like; I'm partial now to having them for breakfast or with afternoon tea. VEGAN

YIELDS APPROXIMATELY 2 DOZEN DONUTS

¼ cup sugar

1½ teaspoons active dry yeast

⅔ cup warm water, brought to 110–115°F

½ cup coconut milk

1¾ cups all-purpose flour

¾ cup rice flour

¾ teaspoon salt

3 tablespoons dried grated coconut (preferably unsweetened)

½–1¼ teaspoons ground green cardamom (see sidebar)

canola, coconut or peanut oil, for frying

salt and confectioners' sugar, to finish

1. This can easily be made in a stand mixer or by hand. In the bowl of a stand mixer fitted with a dough hook, dissolve sugar and yeast in warm water and let bloom 5 to 10 minutes. It should become foamy and frothy. Turn the mixer on low and add coconut milk.

2. In a separate bowl, sift flours together and mix in salt, grated coconut, and cardamom. Add the flour mixture to the mixer and knead on low for 5 to 10 minutes. Conversely, you can also knead by hand—the dough should get pretty smooth (except for the grated coconut) and relatively sticky.

3. Transfer dough to a greased bowl, cover, and let rise for a minimum of 2 hours.

4. On a floured work surface, divide dough into 4 even pieces. Form each piece into a ball and flatten to a disk. Roll each circle out to about ¼" thick and cut using a long knife or a pizza cutter into six triangular pieces. Transfer to a parchment-lined baking sheet.

5. In a Dutch oven or pot, heat 2" to 3" of oil to 360°F. Working in batches, carefully drop a few triangles into the oil. Don't overcrowd or the oil temperature will drop. As soon as the triangles puff, quickly flip them over. This will ensure that both sides cook—if they become lopsided, it will be hard to keep them on the less inflated side to brown. Cook for a few minutes, flipping at intervals until golden brown. Remove to a paper towel–lined plate or baking sheet and lightly salt.

6. Before serving, sprinkle with confectioners' sugar. They are best served immediately and warm, as they can get a touch chewy once they've cooled. If you need to reheat, do so in the oven at a very low temperature.

Traditionally, cardamom is roughly ground and added to the mandazi batter. This results in biting into delightful pieces of cardamom while eating the donuts. I add about 1¼ teaspoons when I'm using roughly ground cardamom, and more like ½ teaspoon when I use the powdered or ground form.

Banana Chocolate Chip Muffins

Okay, so this is a bit of cheating for breakfast. Yes, these are banana chocolate chip muffins, but the reality is that they don't resemble the traditional, dense banana muffins that are usually out there. They are light, fluffy, with a delicate crumb and actually resemble more of a cupcake! Regardless, they are delicious and small, so you won't feel too guilty eating one (or two . . .) first thing in the morning. VEGETARIAN

YIELDS A DOZEN MUFFINS

1 cup all-purpose flour

½ teaspoon baking powder

½ teaspoon baking soda

½ teaspoon salt

1 stick unsalted butter, softened at room temperature

¼ cup cream cheese, softened at room temperature

½ cup light brown or palm sugar

1½ teaspoons vanilla extract

2 eggs, room temperature

¼ cup finely chopped or ground toasted nuts (hazelnuts, walnuts, almonds)

2 overripe bananas, mashed with a fork

½ cup semisweet chocolate chips

1. Preheat the oven to 350°F.

2. In a medium bowl, sift together the flour, baking powder, baking soda, and salt and set aside.

3. To the bowl of a stand mixer with a paddle attachment (you can also use a hand mixer), add the softened butter, cream cheese, sugar, and vanilla. Cream together on a medium speed until light and fluffy.

4. With the mixture on low, add the eggs one at a time, making sure they are incorporated. Add the flour mixture in 3 increments, stopping and scraping down the sides of the bowl between each addition. Carefully, fold in the nuts, mashed bananas, and chocolate chips, again in increments, until the mixture is uniform.

5. Line a muffin tin with paper liners. Use an ice cream scoop to scoop equal amounts of batter into each. Bake on the middle rack of the oven for 20 minutes, until an inserted toothpick comes out clean.

Mushroom and Ajwain Pissaladière

A pissaladière is a Provençal, pizza-like tart, a yeast-based dough typically topped with onions, anchovies, and French oil-cured olives. I love to experiment with toppings, and here I use deeply caramelized onions and fresh, market mushrooms to form the base. Feel free to find your own favorite topping combinations! Instead of making pizza dough from scratch, I like to use puff pastry because it saves time and forms the most perfectly thin, buttery, crunchy layer. I entertain with this recipe because you can precook the topping, assemble, pop it in the oven, and have the most delicious and elegant tart in 15 minutes. I sometimes precut the pastry into little squares before cooking to make it even easier to serve. VEGETARIAN

SERVES 6 AS AN APPETIZER

1 sheet frozen puff pastry, thawed per the package instructions

olive or canola oil, to coat

2½ cups sliced mixed mushrooms (see sidebar)

3 tablespoons unsalted butter, divided

salt, to taste

¼ teaspoon ajwain seeds

¼ teaspoon white cumin seeds

2 medium Spanish onions, thinly sliced

¼ teaspoon red chili flakes

scant ½ teaspoon ground black pepper

scant ½ teaspoon chili powder

scant ½ teaspoon ground cumin

1 egg

1 tablespoon heavy cream

fresh thyme leaves, to taste

1. Preheat oven to 400°F.

2. On a floured surface, roll out puff pastry into an appropriately sized rectangle and place on a baking sheet. I used a 15" × 10" baking sheet, but this dish could be stretched a little farther if your baking sheet is slightly larger. Prick all over with a fork, cover with plastic wrap, and refrigerate until ready to bake.

3. Heat a medium skillet over medium-high heat. Cover bottom of pan with a thin layer of oil and when it starts to shimmer and is about to smoke, add mushrooms and let them just sit for 2 to 3 minutes. This is the best way to truly brown them. Add 1 tablespoon of butter and toss to finish cooking for another minute or two. Season at this point with salt and then remove to a strainer set over a bowl to drain excess liquid and oil.

4. Wipe off skillet and set back over medium heat. Add oil again to coat the bottom of the pan and when oil begins to shimmer, add ajwain and cumin seeds. Fry spices for about a minute, being careful not to burn them. Turn heat down to low, add 2 tablespoons of butter, onions, red chili flakes, black pepper, chili powder, cumin, and a pinch of salt. Cook on low for 20 to 25 minutes, stirring frequently until onions caramelize. Add mushrooms and mix thoroughly. Taste and adjust seasoning. Set mixture aside in a bowl to cool for 10 minutes, using a slotted spoon if necessary to remove any excess liquid.

5. Remove puff pastry from refrigerator and spread mushroom and onion mixture onto pastry, being sure to leave an uncovered edge around the outside. In a small bowl, beat together the egg and heavy cream and brush the uncovered edge with this egg wash. Sprinkle with thyme leaves and bake for 20 to 25 minutes, until the crust is golden brown.

6. Let cool slightly before cutting and serving.

The mushrooms you use here are completely up to your preference. I happen to love the meatiness of shiitakes and the texture of oyster mushrooms. Creminis and portobellos are also fantastic, and if you're feeling fancy, maitakes and porcinis would work beautifully.

Goat Cheese Tart with Mission Figs, Pistachios, and Anise

In the Middle East, figs and anise are often cooked down to a jam. I thought it would be beautiful in a classic fig and goat cheese tart. The pistachios add a gorgeous nuttiness, and I love the combination of sweet and savory here. Of course, I give my favorite tart crust recipe, but feel free to use store-bought if you are in a time pinch. VEGETARIAN

YIELDS (1) 9" ROUND TART OR (1) 13¾" × 4½" RECTANGULAR TART

For the crust:

1½ cups all-purpose flour

1 teaspoon salt

½ teaspoon sugar

1 stick cold, unsalted butter, cut into small cubes

1 egg

1–3 teaspoons water

For the filling:

2 egg yolks

½ cup heavy cream

8 ounces goat cheese

1½ tablespoons freshly squeezed lemon juice

1 teaspoon lemon zest

¾ teaspoon aniseed

1 teaspoon salt

2 tablespoons pistachios, shelled and toasted

10 black mission figs, halved

honey or balsamic vinegar, for drizzling

1. Preheat the oven to 375°F.

2. *For the crust:* In a food processor, pulse together flour, salt, and sugar. Scatter the cold cubes of butter over the dry ingredients and pulse until the butter is cut in and the texture looks like sandy peas or a coarse meal. In a small bowl, lightly beat together the egg and 1 teaspoon of water. Add in increments, pulsing, until the dough sticks together. If the dough still looks dry and doesn't hold together when pinched, pulse in another 1 to 2 teaspoons of water until it does. There will still be a lot of crumbly bits that haven't incorporated—that's okay.

3. Turn the dough out onto a work surface or a piece of parchment paper. LIGHTLY, knead the dough to make sure everything is incorporated. I literally just press it together a bit. Place into plastic wrap and create a flattened disk. Refrigerate for a minimum of 2 to 3 hours (and up to a day).

4. On a floured work surface or in between pieces of parchment paper (with flour), carefully roll out the dough with a rolling pin until uniform thickness and large enough for the round or rectangular tart shell. Carefully transfer to the greased tart shell and press carefully into the sides. Try not to stretch the dough at all. Trim any excess edges and dock or prick holes all over the surface of the dough with a fork. Wrap shell in plastic wrap and freeze for a minimum of a half hour.

5. Remove tart shell from freezer and plastic wrap and place on a baking sheet. Fit a piece of parchment paper on the surface of the dough and weight down with dried beans or baking weights. Bake on the middle rack for 20 minutes. Remove baking weights or beans and parchment paper and bake for another 10 minutes to brown. Let cool slightly.

6. *For the filling:* Turn oven temperature down to 350°F. In a small food processor, process the egg yolks, heavy cream, goat cheese, lemon juice, lemon zest, aniseed, and salt until uniform and smooth. Transfer the cheese mixture to the tart and smooth so it evenly fills the shell. Scatter the pistachios on top of the cheese mixture, and then arrange the fig halves across the tart.

7. Bake for 25 minutes. Serve warm or at room temperature, drizzled with a bit of honey or balsamic.

Guava and Cheese Danishes

Guava paste is used all throughout Latin American cooking. From the Dominican Republic to Colombia to Cuba to Mexico, guavas and guava paste are featured heavily, particularly paired with fresh cheese, often just sliced and layered together. I thought the combo would be divine baked up with some puff pastry for breakfast as a cheese Danish. And so it was . . . . VEGETARIAN

SERVES 6

4 ounces mascarpone, softened

4 ounces cream cheese, softened

¼ cup plus 2 tablespoons confectioners' sugar

1 teaspoon vanilla extract

½ teaspoon ground cinnamon

⅛ teaspoon salt

½ teaspoon lemon zest

1 egg yolk

1 sheet puff pastry, thawed per package instructions

6 (4½" long × ⅛" thick) pieces of guava paste (see sidebar)

1 egg, beaten with 1 to 2 tablespoons heavy cream, for egg wash

1. Preheat the oven to 400°F.

2. In the bowl of a stand mixer or with a hand mixer, combine the mascarpone, cream cheese, confectioners' sugar, vanilla extract, cinnamon, salt, lemon zest, and egg yolk. Use the paddle attachment and cream on low until smooth and uniform.

3. On a floured surface, roll out the thawed puff pastry to approximately 15" × 10". Cut into 6 even (5" × 5") squares. Place about 2 tablespoons or so of the cheese mixture in the center and top with a slice of the guava paste. Fold opposite corners across the cheese and guava, overlapping and securing with a bit of egg wash and pressure. Fold the other corners in but not enough to seal the packet entirely—you just want to create a barrier so the cheese doesn't ooze out during cooking. Brush all exposed surfaces of the pastry with the egg wash.

4. Bake for 20 to 25 minutes, until golden brown. Serve warm or at room temperature.

Guava paste is usually in the ethnic foods aisle of your grocer, by the rest of the Latin products. If you can't find it, you can use another fruit preserve or jam here—strawberry, cherry, red currant, whatever you like! Just spread about 1 to 2 tablespoons of it over the cheese mixture and bake.

Parker House Rolls with Sweet Miso Butter

Making your own Parker rolls is truly satisfying (and oh-so-impressive for your guests). The recipe is easy enough for a baking novice, and yields the most fluffy, buttery rolls out there. The miso butter is the perfect accompaniment—sweet, salty, and nutty—and I used white miso here because it's a bit more mild. If for some outlandish reason you have leftovers, these keep great in the fridge for a few days and make delicious sandwich rolls.

VEGETARIAN

YIELDS 20 ROLLS

For the rolls:

1¼ cups milk

1 (¼-ounce) envelope active dry yeast

2¾ tablespoons sugar

2 tablespoons vegetable shortening

5 tablespoons unsalted butter, room temperature, divided

2 egg yolks

3½ cups all-purpose flour

2½ teaspoons salt

flake salt (like Maldon salt), to finish

For the sweet miso butter:

3 tablespoons unsalted butter, softened at room temperature

2 teaspoons sweet white miso

1. *For the rolls:* In a small saucepan, heat the milk to 110–115°F. Remove from the heat, add the yeast, sugar, shortening, and 2 tablespoons of the butter. Stir to combine and set aside uncovered for 10 minutes.

2. Transfer the milk mixture to a stand mixer fitted with a paddle attachment. Turn the mixer on low and add in the yolks. Combine the flour and salt and add to the mixer. As soon as the dough comes together, change the paddle attachment to the dough hook and knead on low for about 4 to 5 minutes. You can also do this all by hand—mixing the dough together and then kneading on a flat surface for the same amount of time.

3. Gather the dough in a ball and place in a large, greased bowl. Flip so that all sides of the dough are greased, cover with a towel, and let rise for 2 hours.

4. Preheat the oven to 350°F and melt the other 3 tablespoons of butter. Portion the dough into 20 even pieces and roll into roughly 2" balls. Place on a parchment-lined baking sheet and brush with the melted butter. Cover loosely with plastic wrap and set aside to rise for another 30 to 40 minutes.

5. Remove plastic wrap and bake for 25 to 35 minutes, until puffed and golden brown. Brush with any remaining melted butter and sprinkle with the flake salt.

6. *For the sweet miso butter:* Mix together the butter and miso with a spoon until uniform.

7. Serve rolls hot with the sweet miso butter.

If you want to do these in advance or just keep a stash around, after you've formed the dough balls (but before they rise!), you can wrap them in plastic wrap and freeze. You'll want to thaw them, brush with butter, and let rise (about 2 to 2½ hours total) before baking.

Fried "PB&J's"

I distinctly remember my first morning in Turkey, sitting and overlooking the mystic and mind-boggling caves and rock formations of the Cappadocia plateau. I was presented with an elaborate breakfast with Turkish flatbreads (ekmek), cured meats (pastirma and sujuk), and little bowls with different oils, tahini, honey, yogurt, and fruit molasses (pekmez). The combo of grape molasses and tahini slathered on bread, typical for breakfast there, was transformative for me and suddenly became my new version of "pb&j." I had to share it with you.

VEGETARIAN

SERVES 4–6

8 (½") slices of brioche
4–6 tablespoons unsalted butter, divided
3 tablespoons grape or pomegranate molasses (see sidebar)
4 tablespoons tahini
salt, to taste
honey, for drizzling

1. Heat a large skillet over medium heat.

2. Add 2 to 3 tablespoons of butter and let melt. Add 4 slices of the brioche and lightly toast for a few minutes in the pan on both sides. Remove from pan. Repeat using the remaining butter and brioche slices.

3. To assemble sandwiches, spread a heaping 2 teaspoons of molasses on one slice of bread. On the other, generously spread 1 tablespoon of tahini, lightly sprinkle with salt, and drizzle with honey. Fold together and repeat for the remaining sandwiches.

4. Cut each across the diagonal and eat immediately. These are best enjoyed warm so the tahini becomes a bit melted.

Grape or pomegranate molasses can be found at Middle Eastern specialty stores as well as at some traditional grocery stores. If you can't find them, check out my recipe for a homemade version of pomegranate molasses in Chapter 1.

Chapter 9

DESSERTS

My love, my weakness . . . there is nothing like the perfect bite of sweetness to finish a meal.

None of the recipes in this section are strictly traditional. I took flavors, textures, and ingredients I love and turned them on their head. I used baked phyllo dough for a sweet and creamy "bread" pudding studded with summer berries. There's a cake inspired by the Arabic tradition of coffee and dates, and a rich and densely chocolatey loaf made with cinnamon-infused Mexican chocolate.

My favorite dessert, however, has to be my grandmother's fruit spice cake—moist and brandy-scented. This cake is about more than taste—it's about history, love, and is truly an heirloom recipe. Capture your own heirloom recipes to be sure they can be passed down to another generation . . . .

End-of-Summer Bread Pudding (of sorts)

Om Ali is a Lebanese dessert that layers phyllo dough with different nuts, dried fruits, coconut, and a (ridiculously delicious) custard base and has always seemed to me like a Middle Eastern version of bread pudding. At any given point, I tend to have a pack of phyllo sitting in my freezer more often than I have stale bread on hand, so I was inspired to put my own seasonal spin on it. This is now my signature bread pudding, and it's just as rewarding, though slightly more delicate and less carb-heavy than the traditional kind. It's rich, custardy, and I just love the combination of vanilla and berries. I'm big on entertaining with this dessert because it looks beautiful, is elegantly casual, yet is still really easy to throw together. Served warm with a scoop of vanilla ice cream, you'll be hard-pressed to put that spoon down. VEGETARIAN

YIELDS 1 (9") CAKE

8 sheets phyllo dough, thawed per package instructions

1 stick unsalted butter, melted or butter-flavored cooking spray

2 cups milk

2 cups heavy cream

1 cup sugar

1 vanilla bean, split and scraped

1 teaspoon almond extract

pinch salt

2 large eggs, beaten, at room temperature

2 cups mixed berries

1. Preheat the oven to 375°F.

2. Line a large baking sheet with parchment paper and grease the paper. Lay 1 sheet of phyllo on top and brush with melted butter or spray with cooking spray. Lay another on top and repeat the process until all 8 sheets are layered and buttered. You don't have to be too dainty here since they will be broken up for the custard. Bake for 20 minutes, until golden brown, remove, and let cool.

3. In a medium saucepan, combine the milk, heavy cream, sugar, vanilla bean, almond extract, and a pinch of salt and bring up to a strong simmer over medium-high heat. Be careful because it can boil over really easily (has happened to me too many times to count)! Remove from the heat and let steep covered for 10 minutes.

4. Ladle a bit of the hot milk mixture into the beaten eggs and whisk. You want to slowly bring the eggs up to temperature. Keep adding the hot milk, a little bit at a time, whisking in between each addition until the milk and eggs are thoroughly combined.

5. Grease a 9" round cake pan and place on a baking sheet (to catch any juices that might drip). Break the phyllo sheets up into shards. Place half of the shards in the pan, top with 1 cup of the mixed berries, and pour half of the egg/milk mixture on top. Create another layer with the remaining phyllo, berries, and milk mixture.

6. Bake for 25 to 30 minutes, until golden brown and bubbling. Cool a bit before serving but definitely serve warm and preferably with a scoop of vanilla ice cream for a bit more decadence.

Persimmon Tarte Tatin

Persimmons are native to China and Japan, and the biological species name loosely translates to "fruit of the Gods"! Fuyu and Hachiya persimmons are now readily available throughout the United States, and I'm partial to the Fuyus, which are a bit firmer and work well in salads, on their own, or baked into a dessert. Here, they make a great substitute for traditional apples in a tarte tatin, adding their delicate sweetness to the dish. A ripe Fuyu persimmon should be neither too hard nor too soft. Look for firm ones that give a bit when pressed. VEGETARIAN

YIELDS 1 (9" ROUND) PAN

For the crust:

1¼ cups all-purpose flour

½ teaspoon salt

1½ teaspoons sugar

1 stick cold unsalted butter, cut into small cubes

4–5 tablespoons ice water

For the caramel:

¾ cup sugar

3 tablespoons water

1 tablespoon freshly squeezed lemon juice

1 vanilla bean, split and scraped

pinch salt

6 tablespoons unsalted butter

2 Fuyu persimmons, peeled and sliced thinly into ⅛" thick

crème fraîche, for garnish

1. Preheat oven to 400°F. Grease and line a 9" cake pan with a parchment round in the bottom.

2. *For the crust*: Pulse the flour, salt, and sugar together in a food processor until combined. Sprinkle the cold butter over top and pulse until the mixture resembles a coarse meal. Pulse in the water, 1 tablespoon at a time, until the dough sticks together when pressed. Form the dough into a disk; wrap with plastic wrap and refrigerate for at least 30 minutes.

3. *For the caramel*: In a small saucepan, add sugar, water, lemon juice, vanilla bean, and salt. Melt over medium heat until all the sugar is dissolved and sugar mixture has become a medium caramel color. Reduce heat to low and carefully add butter, one pat at a time, using a heatproof rubber spatula to stir and incorporate after each addition.

4. Pour ¾ of the caramel into the greased and lined cake pan. Layer the persimmons in an overlapping, circular pattern, being careful not to touch the hot caramel. Add the remaining caramel over the persimmons and set aside.

5. On a floured surface, roll out the pastry dough into ¼" thickness. Using the cake pan as a guide, trim the dough with a 1" border around the cake pan. Layer the pastry dough into the cake pan on top of the caramel and persimmons. Tuck the excess dough under the layer of dough, and bake for 25 to 30 minutes.

6. Cool for at least an hour. Run a knife around the edge of the tart, invert, and serve. If it sticks, gently warm the pan over a low flame before inverting. Garnish with a little crème fraîche.

Mexican Chocolate Loaf Cake

I have a serious love affair going on with Mexican chocolate, the deliciously sugary, cinnamon-y, thick tablets of sweet dark chocolate. Once I discovered it, I went on a Mexican chocolate rampage, sneaking it into desserts whenever I could and even going so far as to add it to my morning coffee on occasion (ridiculous, I know). A pastry chef I work with looked down his nose when I told him I was doing a loaf cake, but I adore them! Loaf cakes are unassuming and, when decadent enough like this one, an unexpected bite of seemingly casual luxury. This one is rich and moist, with melted bites of Mexican chocolate and that kick of cinnamon. VEGETARIAN

YIELDS 1 (9½") LOAF

1¼ cups all-purpose flour

⅔ cup Dutch process cocoa powder (see sidebar)

1 teaspoon cinnamon

¾ teaspoon baking powder

½ teaspoon baking soda

¾ teaspoon salt

2 sticks unsalted butter, softened at room temperature

¾ cup crème fraîche, softened at room temperature

1 cup dark brown sugar

¼ cup white sugar

2 large eggs, at room temperature

2 teaspoons vanilla extract

8 ounces Mexican chocolate, chopped finely (see sidebar)

confectioners' sugar, for garnish

1. Preheat the oven to 350°F. Butter and lightly flour the loaf pan and set aside.

2. In a bowl, sift together the flour, cocoa powder, cinnamon, baking powder, baking soda, and salt.

3. Fit a stand mixer with the paddle attachment or use a hand mixer, and cream together the butter, crème fraîche, and the sugars until light and fluffy using a medium speed. Stop and scrape down the sides of the bowl to make sure everything is fully incorporated. With the mixer back on, add the eggs one at a time and the vanilla extract.

4. Reduce the speed on the mixer and add ⅓ of the flour mixture followed by ⅓ of the chocolate. Repeat twice and then scrape down. Mix again briefly only so that the batter is just uniform—be careful not to overmix.

5. Transfer batter to the loaf pan and bake for 60 to 70 minutes, until a toothpick comes out clean when inserted. Let cool on a rack before unmolding—run a thin knife along the sides if it's sticking a bit. Serve garnished with confectioners' sugar.

I use Dutch process cocoa powder because it's more mellow, less bitter, and less acidic than traditional cocoa powder and really lets the Mexican chocolate flavor come through. Mexican chocolate is found in the ethnic or baking aisle of many grocery stores as well as at Latin, specialty, and gourmet markets. If you can't find any, substitute a good-quality semisweet chocolate and throw in another teaspoon of cinnamon.

Hot Coffee-Glazed Medjool Date Cakes

I had the great fortune of staying with a dear friend of mine in Bahrain. She has an amazing family, and I was swooped up into the daily routine, happily learning Middle Eastern dishes by her side in the kitchen. One tradition I really loved was the afternoon Arabic coffee with dates. The coffee was strong, scented with cardamom, and the dates, plump and sweet, came straight from her own trees in the backyard. I tried to replicate that taste memory here, in these sweet little cakes. VEGETARIAN

YIELDS 8 (3" ROUND) CAKES

For the date cakes:
½ pound Medjool dates, pitted (approximately 12–13 dates)
1¾ cups water
3 tablespoons instant espresso powder
1 vanilla bean, split and scraped
1 teaspoon ground cardamom
1 teaspoon salt
1 stick unsalted butter, softened at room temperature
¾ cup light brown sugar
4 eggs, room temperature
1¾ cups all-purpose flour
1½ teaspoons baking soda

For the coffee glaze:
2 tablespoons water
1½ teaspoons instant espresso powder
1½ teaspoons coffee liqueur
¼ teaspoon vanilla extract
¾ cup confectioners' sugar

1. Preheat the oven to 350°F.

2. *For the date cakes:* In a medium saucepan, combine the dates, water, espresso powder, vanilla bean, cardamom, and salt. Bring up to a boil, remove from the heat, cover, and steep for 15 minutes. Transfer to a blender and purée until smooth. Cool to room temperature.

3. Using the paddle attachment on a stand mixer or with a hand mixer, cream together the butter and the sugar on low speed. With the mixer still going, add the eggs, one at a time, stopping to scrape down the sides of the bowl and making sure each egg is incorporated before adding the next. Sift together the flour and baking soda and add to the butter mixture in increments, ⅓ at a time. Stop the mixer, scrape down, turn the mixer back on low, and add in the cooled date purée. You want it just incorporated—don't overmix.

4. Place eight 3" cylindrical paper molds on a baking sheet. Fill with the batter only a little more than halfway—it rises quite a bit. Bake for 25 to 30 minutes on the center rack in the oven, until a cake tester comes out clean. Remove and place on a rack to cool.

5. *For the coffee glaze:* Bring all ingredients up to a boil and then lower to a simmer. Simmer uncovered for 3 to 4 minutes, until the glaze is thick and a bit syrupy. Glaze the cakes while the glaze and the cakes are still hot.

6. Serve warm or at room temperature.

If you're thinking Medjool dates probably belong in trail mix, stop right there! These dates are large, sweet, and basically melt in your mouth. Close your eyes while eating them and you will taste caramel and chocolate.

Food Is Giving

When I host a dinner party, there's something I don't tell the guests. You see, I have this habit, or skill, some may call it, of being able to watch using peripheral vision and other means of subterfuge each and every guest and know just what (and how much of it) they ate. There, it's out.

But it goes even further than that. I know at restaurants for a table of 12 or even 14 of us, who ordered what appetizers and what entrées, and I direct the servers accordingly when they get mixed up (to some of my friends' surprise). I notice likes, dislikes, allergies—I will forget a friend's middle name but remember how much she enjoyed a dish she ate on one of her travels. I listen to people's childhood stories and make mental notes of the dishes that shaped them growing up. Lastly, and I'm not completely proud of this one, I notice when there are wrappers in the trash at home, when my husband has eaten something when he says he's on a diet and refuses my fatty meal to snack on a cookie or some other worthless caloric expenditure (compared to my meal!).

You see, I grew up with family being all up in your business and, particularly, in your food business. Moms, aunts, and grandmas watched, dare I say *patrolled*, what you ate. Not eating was an insult, and additional helpings were heaped on plates despite any desire to the contrary. You couldn't say no—it wasn't even a possibility. The reverse is true as well—to feed was to give and so to not feed was equally insulting. It would drive me insane when, on the off chance I did ask for another helping, that half scoop of rice would always end up being two to three times the amount I wanted on my plate. The idea of running out of food was offensive, something you could never live down and might bring up for years to come. The odd correlative to all of this would be an unparalleled lack of tact or restraint in commenting on your physique or a few extra pounds, and so the mantra would be "eat but stay slim or we will talk about you."

The insane thing about it all is that instead of bucking the system, instead of revolting against this torturous ideology, I've adopted it (except any judgment on weight gain)! I've bought into it all . . . I too feel insulted when people don't eat my food. And I *always* serve (and heap on people's plates) way more than anyone wants or possibly can fit in his or her stomach. I guess at the end of the day, it's not a terrible tradition to take on, and it reinforces what might be the underlying truth to it all: food is giving.

Meyer Lemon Cream with "Amarena-Style" Cherries

Traditionally, a custard has to be baked or stirred on the stovetop and requires delicate handling of eggs or yolks (no scrambling!) to achieve a silky, thick texture. This one doesn't and couldn't be easier. The lemon juice actually "sets" the cream and does the work for you—thickening up as it cools in the fridge. I used seasonal, Meyer lemons here because they have that gorgeous mandarin-lemon sweetness and are very easy to juice. Amarena cherries are my favorite—sour cherries from the Emilia-Romagna region in Italy, preserved in a secret syrup. They also happen to be quite expensive and not the easiest to find, so I devised my own preserve using dried, pitted sour cherries. The Meyer lemon-cherry combo is heavenly, and this easy do-ahead dessert is perfect for weeknights or entertaining. VEGETARIAN, GLUTEN-FREE

SERVES 6

For the Meyer lemon cream:
2½ cups heavy cream
1 vanilla bean, split and scraped
¼ teaspoon salt
¼ cup sugar
3 tablespoons honey
1 tablespoon Meyer (or regular) lemon zest
½ cup freshly squeezed Meyer (or regular) lemon juice

For the "Amarena-style" cherries:

½ cup sugar

½ cup cherry juice or water

2 teaspoons freshly squeezed lemon juice

1 stick cinnamon

½ teaspoon vanilla extract

pinch salt

3 tablespoons Amaretto liqueur

¼ pound dried, pitted sour cherries

1. *For the Meyer lemon cream:* In a small saucepan, bring heavy cream, vanilla bean, salt, sugar, honey, and lemon zest up to a boil. Remove from the heat, cover, and let steep for 20 minutes. Gently stir in lemon juice and strain cream mixture. Transfer into individual ramekins and refrigerate for a minimum of 5 hours, until thickened and chilled through. These can be made a day or two ahead of time.

2. *For the "Amarena-style" cherries:* Bring all ingredients up to a boil and reduce to a simmer. Simmer uncovered for 7 to 10 minutes, until the liquid reduces and becomes syrupy. It should coat a spoon but will also thicken as it cools. Refrigerate until chilled.

3. Serve the chilled Meyer lemon cream topped with a small spoonful of the cherries.

Salted Caramels with Sweet Garam Masala

Homemade confections are so much fun when you are entertaining. These salted caramels are sinfully easy to make but are really impressive when finished. The garam masala and vanilla bean add depth of flavor, and of course, the salty-sweet combo is delicious.

VEGETARIAN, GLUTEN-FREE

YIELDS 70–80 (½") CARAMELS

1 cup heavy cream

5 tablespoons unsalted butter, room temperature, cut into cubes

1 vanilla bean, split and scraped

½ teaspoon salt

½ teaspoon ground garam masala

½ cup honey

1¼ cups sugar

flaky sea salt (Maldon), to finish

1. Line a 9" × 5" loaf pan with foil and grease.

2. In a medium saucepan, bring up to a boil the heavy cream with butter, vanilla bean, salt, and garam masala. Remove from the heat.

3. In a large saucepan, heat honey and sugar over medium-high heat to 280°F. I stir just in the beginning, using a heatproof spatula to combine and then brushing down the sugar on the sides with a wet pastry brush.

4. Strain in the heavy cream mixture carefully—it will bubble and spatter a bit (that's why you want a large saucepan). Continue to cook this mixture until it reaches 250°F.

5. Pour into the prepared loaf pan and cool at room temperature for a half hour. Transfer to the fridge for a minimum of 2 hours.

6. Transfer hardened caramel to a cutting board and sprinkle the top with the Maldon salt. Cut as desired—if it's been in the fridge longer than 2 hours, you may need to let it come closer to room temperature before you'll be able to cut them.

7. Store the caramels individually wrapped or spaced apart (they tend to stick together!) in an airtight container at room temperature. They should keep for 3 to 4 weeks.

Grandmother's Tribute

My parents came to visit me one weekend, and my mom brought me the most incredible surprise—her mother's original recipes (what she could find). They were written in her own handwriting, complete with *mugs* as her measurement for *cups* and all sorts of other short-hand. We sat down and had a long chat about my late grandmother—her life, successes, tendencies, and habits, her love of cooking, and her deep obsession with her garden. It was stunning nostalgia—a bit cathartic for both of us and definitely a beautiful moment that I will always cherish.

And I have to say I was a bit rocked by some of the things I heard! When you get to know your grandparents as a child, it's just such a different and, quite frankly, incomplete perspective. I do remember her killer fried chicken, handing out (i.e., rationing) dark chocolates, and the constant jingling of her wrist . . . . But she was also a skilled baker, created her own flavor combinations (crème caramel with saffron and cardamom was a specialty!), was maniacal about Japanese-style flower arranging, and loved throwing parties even though it gave her a ton of anxiety—all this replete with full sari, hair, and makeup *and* in the mother country.

Grandmothers to me are the epicenter, the trailblazers. They are the folks who truly care about history and bring family together. They pass on tradition, teach and cook for no other reason than it is their identity, their way of leaving their mark on this world. When it comes to my grandmothers (and I include my husband's grandmothers here because, for me, family is family), each of their stories is so unique and persevering—their strength, their courage in the face of hardship, and, most importantly, their love constantly reminds me of whom I want to be and how I want to leave my own mark.

I am always channeling the memory of the amazing women that came before me in the kitchen. Just like they did, I try to make food and dishes my own, create my own "secrets," and pass on traditions the way that I know how. Whether it's Rosy's Beef and Potato Patties, Gran's Peas and Rice, or Nani's Fruit Spice Cake, their food succeeds them, is timeless and indelible, and will forever be treasured, as will they.

Nani's Fruit Spice Cake

My grandmother was renowned for her fruit spice cake. This is something she made all the time for my mom and her sisters, and I've been told the smell of the sweet spices wafting through the house would drive everyone crazy with anticipation! I always make it for the holidays—it makes me stop and remember my family (isn't that what the holidays are for?) and the trailblazing women that came before me. My favorite way to serve this cake is a bit warm with a crème anglaise or even a dollop of vanilla ice cream. Thank you, Nani, for passing down this beautiful cake recipe. VEGETARIAN

YIELDS 1 (9") CAKE

For the cake:

⅓ cup unsalted, raw almonds

⅓ cup unsalted pistachios, shelled

⅓ cup walnuts

1 cup all-purpose flour

½ cup semolina flour

2¼ teaspoons baking powder

½ teaspoon baking soda

1½ teaspoons salt

1½ teaspoons ground cinnamon

1½ teaspoons ground cardamom

1½ teaspoons ground ginger

¾ teaspoon ground nutmeg

pinch ground cloves

¾ cup mixed peel, chopped finely

¾ cup golden raisins

¼ cup dried plums, chopped finely

¼ cup dried apricots, chopped finely

1¾ cups sugar, divided

¼ cup water

¼ cup milk, brandy, or rum

1 stick plus 7 tablespoons unsalted butter, softened at room temperature

5 eggs, room temperature

For the apricot glaze:

½ cup apricot preserves

1 tablespoon water

1. Preheat oven to 325°F.

2. *For the cake:* To the bowl of a food processor, add almonds, pistachios, and walnuts. Pulse until the texture becomes like a fine meal—you want the nuts to have a bit of texture but without any large pieces.

3. To a medium bowl, sift together the flours, baking powder, baking soda, salt, and ground spices. In another bowl, add the mixed peel, raisins, dried plums, and apricots and toss with a bit of the flour mixture. Coat the fruits in flour—this will help suspend the fruit in the mixture and prevent it all from sinking to the bottom of the pan.

4. In a small, nonstick saucepan, melt ¼ cup of sugar over medium heat and heat until the sugar caramelizes. You want to achieve a deep amber color, but be careful not to let it burn. As soon as it turns amber, remove from the heat and add the ¼ cup of water as well as the ¼ cup of milk, brandy, or rum to stop the cooking. Caramel gets very hot, so be careful not to splash when you add the liquids. If some of the caramel hardens up, gently heat the mixture until it's a uniform syrup.

5. In a stand mixer or using a hand mixer on low, cream together the butter with 1½ cups of sugar until light and fluffy. Add the eggs one at a time, beating to incorporate each time. Alternating, add ⅓ of the flour mixture and ⅓ of the caramel mixture until both are used up. Stop, scrape down the sides of the bowl, and give it one more mix—you just want the flour to incorporate. Fold in the floured fruits by hand.

6. Immediately, pour the batter into a greased, floured, parchment-lined springform pan and bake on the middle rack for 1 hour. Let cool slightly before turning out—you may need to run your knife along the sides to loosen the cake, but it should pop out nicely.

7. *For the apricot glaze:* In a small saucepan over medium heat, whisk together the apricot preserves and the water until uniform. Brush the cooled cake with the glaze before cutting and serving.

My grandmother was really particular about her cakes. When my mom and her sisters would help her bake, she would only let them stir or mix in one direction! Overmixing was another pet peeve—it causes the cake to toughen up, so mix only until the flour is just incorporated for a tender crumb.

South African Milk Tart with Fruits

I tried a really delicious milk tart a few years back when I was visiting Capetown and was hooked! This is one of those ubiquitous desserts in South Africa that's served throughout the country, on all sorts of occasions, and every cook has his or her own secrets. Melktart (meaning, literally, milk tart) is a tradition that came from the Dutch settlers in the country. The filling here is basically a pastry cream with hints of cinnamon, almond, and (my addition) vanilla. The cornstarch helps to thicken the cream and to make sure it's not too egg-y, and the beaten egg whites lighten the batter and add an airy quality to the finished product. The fruit topping isn't traditional, but I thought it worked beautifully with the pastry cream–like filling. VEGETARIAN

YIELDS 1 (9") FLUTED TART

For the crust:

½ package frozen puff pastry (1 sheet), defrosted

1 egg, beaten with a bit of heavy cream, for egg wash

For the filling:

1½ cups whole milk

½ teaspoon salt

1 stick cinnamon

1 vanilla bean, split and scraped

½ teaspoon almond essence

½ cup heavy cream

¼ cup cornstarch

1½ tablespoons unsalted butter

2 eggs, separated

½ cup plus 2 tablespoons confectioners' sugar, divided

½ teaspoon ground cinnamon

For the topping:

Sliced or whole fruit of choice: strawberries, blueberries, raspberries, kumquats, cape gooseberries, etc.

1. Preheat the oven to 375°F.

2. *For the crust:* Start by rolling out and blind-baking the crust. On a floured surface, roll the sheet of puff pastry out just enough so it will cover the inside of the tart pan and have some overlap. Place it carefully in the tart shell and press it into the corners and sides. Trim the excess. Place a piece of wax paper across the top of the tart so it covers the sides. Add dried beans to weigh down the crust and refrigerate for 15 minutes while you start on the filling.

3. Place in the oven and bake for 20 minutes. Take the crust out of the oven, remove the weights, and brush with the egg wash. Put back in the oven for another 5 minutes until golden. Set aside until ready to fill and leave the oven on.

4. *For the filling:* In a small saucepan, bring the milk, salt, cinnamon stick, vanilla bean, and almond essence up to boil. Lower immediately to a simmer. In a small bowl, whisk together the heavy cream with the cornstarch, making sure there aren't any lumps. Add this to the milk mixture along with the butter and stir until the mixture thickens. Remove from the heat.

5. Put the egg yolks in a larger bowl because you'll be adding the milk mixture to them. You want to start by adding a little bit of the milk mixture and stirring or whisking to incorporate. Continue to do this a little at a time until the milk mixture is completely incorporated—we do this to avoid cooking the yolks and having bits of it in the tart. Let this mixture cool to closer to body temperature before moving on to the next step.

6. In another bowl, beat the egg whites with the ½ cup of confectioners' sugar until soft peaks form—it should be light and fluffy. Add a spoonful or two of the milk custard to the egg whites and incorporate. Carefully, fold the egg whites into the milk custard to lighten it up. Be careful not to overmix or you will deflate it significantly.

7. Add this filling to the tart shell. Mix together the last 2 tablespoons of confectioners' sugar with cinnamon and sprinkle on top of the tart. This will develop into a nice brown crust on top.

8. Bake for 10 minutes, then lower the temperature 25° to 350°F, and bake another 15 minutes.

9. Cool on a rack and top with fruits of your choice before serving. As a fruit tart, I like this on the cold side, but if you forgo the fruits, this can be served warm.

Espresso-Chocolate Brigadeiros

Brigadeiros, docinhos or sweets that are enjoyed all over the country, are one of my favorite Brazilian discoveries. These are little balls of luscious milk fudge that are easy to make and can be layered with any flavor combo you like. These can be as simple as three ingredients—sweetened condensed milk, unsalted butter, and whatever you are garnishing them with—but I love the chocolate ones. I use real chocolate here in lieu of just cocoa (the tradition) to give it a much richer taste, and I also use a touch of espresso powder, which, I think, brings out what's best about the semisweet chocolate. This version is somewhere between a truffle and a brigadeiro—but the result is simply heavenly: rich, thick fudgy bites with that signature mocha flavor. VEGETARIAN, GLUTEN-FREE

YIELDS 2 DOZEN BRIGADEIROS

3 tablespoons unsalted butter

1 (14-ounce) can sweetened condensed milk

¼ teaspoon salt

3 tablespoons heavy cream

1 teaspoon light corn syrup

½ teaspoon vanilla extract

1¼ teaspoons instant espresso powder

1 teaspoon unsweetened cocoa powder

3½ ounces semisweet or bittersweet chocolate, chopped (approximately ¾ cup)

cocoa powder, chocolate sprinkles or vermicelli, and/or
chocolate-covered espresso beans, for garnish

1. In a small, preferably nonstick pot, melt the butter over medium-low heat. Add the sweetened condensed milk, salt, heavy cream, corn syrup, and vanilla extract and whisk to combine. When the mixture starts to bubble, add the espresso powder, cocoa powder, and chopped chocolate and whisk to melt chocolate. Cook on medium-low for 10 to 15 minutes, whisking constantly. The mixture should just lightly bubble around the edges, so reduce the heat if it's cooking too quickly.

2. When it's ready, the mixture will pull away from the sides and slide around the bottom. Transfer to a metal bowl and don't scrape the bottom of the pot. Let cool for 30 to 45 minutes at room temperature. Cover with plastic wrap and transfer to the fridge.

3. Cool the mixture completely before rolling the brigadeiros. This will take likely between 3 and 4 hours. I actually took the bowl out after 2 hours and used a small, greased ice cream scoop to scoop out 24 equal mounds of the mixture onto a parchment-lined baking sheet. Then, I put the mounds back into the fridge to firm up for another 20 minutes. The increased surface area makes it cool faster.

4. Make sure your hands are greased and roll the mixture into even-sized balls. Then, it is up to your imagination how to garnish. You can simply roll in cocoa powder or sprinkles. I garnished mine with chocolate vermicelli and a chocolate-covered espresso bean. I think little paper baking cups make them look adorable. These are best enjoyed at room temperature.

These will keep for 2 days at room temperature if you keep them in an airtight container. In the fridge, they'll keep for closer to a month. If refrigerating, remember to bring to room temperature before serving.

Hibiscus Paletas

Paletas are basically Latin American frozen pops. They are usually made with water and fresh fruit or vegetable juice, sometimes with bits of fruit, or they can be milk-based. Although hibiscus is often used for paletas, I took a cue from a West Indian drink called sorrel, a sweetened hibiscus drink scented with cinnamon and cloves, and spiced them up a bit. These are the perfect cool and easy summer treat.

VEGAN, GLUTEN-FREE

YIELDS 3¼ CUPS, OR APPROXIMATELY 6–8 POPSICLES

3 cups water

1 cup dried hibiscus flowers

1 cinnamon stick

4 whole cloves

1 cup sugar

1. In a medium pot, bring all ingredients up to a boil. Remove from the heat, cover, and let steep for 20 minutes. Let cool to room temperature.

2. Strain liquid, using the back of a spoon against the hibiscus flowers to push through as much liquid as possible.

3. Pour strained liquid into Popsicle molds and let freeze until solid (about 7 to 8 hours).

Shrikhand with Strawberries and Balsamic Caramel

When I was travelling in Goa, I discovered shrikhand, a sweetened, thickened yogurt scented with cardamom, saffron, and even mango, that's usually eaten with fried Indian bread called puris. I was addicted to the stuff and would keep going back to the fridge to take spoonfuls of it until it all mysteriously disappeared. To me, the texture of shrikhand is somewhere between a panna cotta and a budino—thick, luscious, and creamy. I am not always a yogurt person—I have to be in the mood for that tang—but through the hanging process and sweetening, this yogurt transforms and becomes lusciously mild. I use corn syrup to sweeten it here because I find sugar breaks down the yogurt a bit and, untraditionally, a bit of crème fraîche to add body. Paired with the balsamic caramel, strawberries, and a bit of crunch from the almonds, it's positively sinful. VEGETARIAN, GLUTEN-FREE

SERVES 4–6

For the shrikhand:
1 quart full-fat Greek yogurt
¼ cup crème fraîche
½ cup plus 2 tablespoons light corn syrup
⅛ teaspoon lemon zest
½ teaspoon roughly ground cardamom
generous pinch salt

For the balsamic caramel:
¼ cup sugar
2 tablespoons water
¼ cup balsamic vinegar
½ teaspoon vanilla extract
pinch salt
½ pound strawberries, hulled and thinly sliced
toasted almond slices, for garnish

1. *For the shrikhand:* The first step is to thicken the yogurt by hanging it overnight in cheesecloth and letting the liquid drip out from it. Line a medium bowl with a large square of cheesecloth with about 2" of overhang on all sides. Then, just turn out the yogurt into the lined bowl and tie the ends of the cheesecloth up to form a knot, squeezing the yogurt a bit. Take the top of the cheesecloth, tie it to a wooden spoon, and lay the spoon over the top of a medium stockpot. Refrigerate overnight, making sure the yogurt bundle is clearing the bottom of the pot, and all the liquid will simply drip out.

2. Transfer the hung yogurt to a large bowl or to the bowl of a stand mixer. Add the crème fraîche and whip until uniform and a bit fluffy. Add the corn syrup, lemon zest, cardamom, and salt and continue whipping until all of the ingredients are evenly distributed.

3. *For the balsamic caramel:* In a small saucepan, heat the sugar and water over medium-high heat. Watch the mixture as the sugar dissolves, thickens, and then starts to caramelize. Sugar can go from a lovely caramel to a burnt mess very quickly, so keep an eye on it.

4. When the sugar starts to caramelize, gently stir using a heatproof spatula to help create an even color. Once the color reaches a deep amber, add the balsamic vinegar, vanilla, and salt. Be careful because the caramel is *extremely* hot and can spatter! Let the mixture thicken on the heat for another 1 to 2 minutes, until the caramel coats a spoon; remove from heat, and let cool completely.

5. Serve shrikhand chilled, topped with sliced strawberries; drizzle with the balsamic caramel, and sprinkle a few toasted almonds on top.

For the balsamic caramel, I used a technique in French cooking called *gastrique*, or *agro-dolce* in Italian cooking, which reduces a mixture of any acid (vinegar, lemon or orange juice, etc.) with sugar and other ingredients and is often served as a sauce with seafood, poultry, or meat. I took the sugar further on its own first to a deep amber state and then added a high quality balsamic to create a rich caramel sauce. Have fun and experiment with your own caramels or *gastriques*!

Chapter 10

DRINKS

I love to entertain with creative cocktails and nonalcoholic beverages alike, and here are some of my favorites. My rum punch is one of the most authentic out there and sneaks up on everyone that has it. I especially love my Black Plum and Hibiscus "Sangria." This is a full-flavored nonalcoholic version that also tastes amazing with a splash of red wine and brandy. And finally, an aromatic coffee straight from the streets of Zanzibar. Whether you are capping off a meal or relaxing in the sun, I hope you enjoy these sips as much as I do.

Cape Gooseberry Sour

The basic Peruvian Pisco Sour is delicious, but I've experienced one with cape gooseberries, an Aguaymento Sour, where they muddle them in Pisco overnight to produce an aguaymento liquor. I am a cape goose-berry fan—they are lightly tart and sweet with a texture closer to a cherry tomato than a berry. What I find interesting is their muskiness— it's like a honeyed, floral quality—and I slice them for my fruit tart (see South African Milk Tart with Fruits in Chapter 9), make them into preserves, and love them in this cocktail. This cocktail is inspired by the Aguaymento Sour, but I use tequila here and blend up the gooseberries instead of soaking them. When my girlfriends come by (and cape goose-berries are in season), this is what I make them. VEGETARIAN

4 MARTINIS

2 pints cape gooseberries, paper husks removed and washed, reserving 4 cape gooseberries with husk for garnish

1 cup tequila

½ cup simple syrup (equal parts water and sugar dissolved over modest heat; cool to room temperature before using)

½ cup lime juice (preferably fresh, reserving a half-cut lime)

2 egg whites

cinnamon sugar, for rim

1. In a blender, combine the cape gooseberries, tequila, simple syrup, lime juice, and egg whites and blend on high for a minute or so, until the gooseberries are pulverized. You can strain at this point, but I like to leave it with texture so I can taste little bits of the gooseberries.

2. Run the half-cut lime around the rim of the martini glasses and dip them into a dish with the cinnamon sugar.

3. Transfer cape gooseberry mixture to a martini shaker with ice (working in batches), shake, and pour evenly into the martini glasses.

4. Slice the 4 cape gooseberries halfway through and garnish the martini glasses with them. Enjoy!

Cape gooseberries are also called ground cherries. They are native to South America but are also grown in the UK and South Africa. They are cousins of the tomatillo, which you can tell in both their husks and texture. Check out your local farmers' market in the late summer and early fall to find them.

Melon Horchata

Mexican horchata has its roots in Spain and belongs to a class of drinks called aqua frescas, literally "fresh waters," made with different ingredients like fruits, nuts, and grains. The basic version is made with rice and cinnamon, but often almonds, sesame seeds, barley, cocoa beans, or coconut are included. I went with a fruit version here using melon because I love to drink this in the summer, but there are so many combinations you can play with. And if it's that kind of party, you can always add in the optional rum . . . .

VEGAN, GLUTEN-FREE

SERVES 4–6 (YIELDS APPROXIMATELY 1 QUART)

½ cup long grain rice

1 cinnamon stick

2 cups hot water

1 (2½–3-pound) cantaloupe, peeled, seeded, and cut into a medium dice (approximately 4 cups)

½ cup sugar

½ teaspoon vanilla extract

½ cup rum (optional)

ground cinnamon, to garnish

1. In a blender, purée the rice and cinnamon stick with hot water and let sit for 3 hours at room temperature or overnight in the fridge.

2. Blend again with the diced melon, sugar, and vanilla extract. Strain through a fine sieve, add rum if using, and chill thoroughly.

3. Stir horchata if there's any separation and serve over ice, sprinkled with a bit of cinnamon. The horchata should last for about 4 to 5 days in the fridge.

You can substitute honeydew, watermelon, or even berries for the cantaloupe as alternatives or simply use 2 cups water in its place if you want to try the traditional version.

Frozen Limonada

Almost every culture has its form of lemonade, and the word limonada *is actually used in a number of different languages. This version is a frozen, granita-like version that is Middle Eastern–inspired, with a bit of depth from orange blossom water and some fresh mint.* VEGAN, GLUTEN-FREE

SERVES 4–6

1¼ cups sugar

1 (2") piece of lemon peel

5¼ cups water, divided

2 cups freshly squeezed lemon juice (from approximately 12–14 lemons)

3–4 tablespoons orange blossom water

small handful of mint (optional)

1. Combine sugar, lemon peel, and 1¼ cups water in a small saucepan. Bring up to boil over medium-high heat, whisking to dissolve sugar. Remove from the heat, cover, and let sit for 15 minutes. You want to infuse the simple syrup with the lemon flavor. Remove peel and chill completely.

2. Mix lemon juice with the chilled simple syrup, remaining 4 cups water, orange blossom water, and mint, if using. Transfer to a baking dish and place in the freezer. You are starting a granita process, and the thinner the layer of lemonade, the more quickly it will freeze. After 2 hours, remove the baking dish and, using a fork, scrape the ice crystals to form an icy texture. Place back in the freezer and repeat again after an hour.

3. Transfer the mixture to a food processor and process to make a slushy. Work in batches if necessary and enjoy immediately!

Pink Grapefruit Paloma

This is a simple, refreshing Mexican cocktail I love more than the margarita. It's 3 ingredients and a salt rim, so it doesn't get easier. If you can't find any grapefruit soda, simply mix (preferably fresh) grapefruit juice with a little seltzer or club soda to your taste. VEGAN

SERVES 4–6

3 cups grapefruit soda
½ cup lime juice
1 cup tequila or mezcal
wedges of lime and salt for rim

1. In a pitcher, mix together the grapefruit soda, lime juice, and tequila or mezcal.
2. Run the lime wedge around the glasses and dip them into a dish with salt.
3. Serve over ice, in the salt-rimmed glasses with a lime wedge.

St. Lucian Rum Punch

Each island lays claim over inventing the original rum punch, but this version I tasted down in St. Lucia is by far my favorite! It's light, fruity, has complexity from the spices and the bitters, and goes down easy. This rum punch has quickly become my signature warm weather cocktail, and I usually just have a pitcher of it ready in my fridge during the summer for the friends that stop by (see the note on aging, not you or I but the punch!). Don't let the light taste fool you—it will sneak up on you after a few sips!

VEGAN, GLUTEN-FREE

SERVES 10–12

3 cups orange juice

3 cups pineapple juice

1 cup lime juice

generous pinch cinnamon

generous pinch nutmeg

6 healthy shakes of angostura bitters

2½ cups dark or light rum

grenadine syrup, to taste

1¼ cups simple syrup (see recipe in this chapter)

1. In a large bowl or pitcher, mix together juices, spices, bitters, and rum. Add grenadine syrup until the punch reaches the color of a flaming sunset.

2. Grenadine syrups differ in sweetness, so I like to add the simple syrup after this point and taste along the way to make sure it's not too sweet.

3. Serve over ice.

This tastes great immediately, but the flavors meld and get better as it sits, so I like to make this a few hours to a day (or two) and "age" my rum punch in advance of serving.

Cherry-Yuzu Champagne Floaters

I am a huge fan of yuzu in drinks! Yuzu is a Japanese citrus that has notes of lime, grapefruit, and mandarin along with a floral muskiness and a bit of salinity. I throw it into my daily seltzer, vodka cocktails, and even lemonade. (Yuzu is sold at specialty Asian markets and can also be found online.) It balances out sweetness perfectly and that's why I paired it with a cherry sorbet here. The combination marries beautifully with the fruity fizz of a champagne or prosecco and also happens to turn your drink into this lovely rose shade. VEGAN, GLUTEN-FREE

SERVES 6

1 tablespoon yuzu juice
1 bottle champagne or prosecco, chilled
6 small scoops cherry sorbet
mint leaves, for garnish

1. To each champagne flute, add ½ teaspoon of yuzu juice.

2. Top with the champagne and then a small scoop of cherry sorbet. Be careful not to fill the glasses too full before adding the sorbet as it fizzes a bit when it's added.

3. Serve immediately, garnished with mint leaves.

Thyme-Green Tea Cocktail

This is another drink you can keep in a pitcher in the fridge for easy, warm weather entertaining. Iced green tea forms the base and is sweetened with a thyme-infused simple syrup. A touch of lemon juice adds acidity to result in a light, refreshing drink that's great with or without the vodka. VEGAN, GLUTEN-FREE

SERVES 6–8

For the thyme simple syrup:
¾ cup water
¾ cup sugar
10 sprigs of thyme

For the cocktail:
4 cups cold, brewed green tea
⅔ cup freshly squeezed lemon juice
1½ tablespoons yuzu or lime juice
1¼ cups vodka

1. *For the thyme simple syrup:* In a small saucepan, heat the water, sugar, and thyme over medium-high heat, stirring until the water comes up to a boil. Remove from the heat, cover, and let steep for 15 minutes. Strain and cool.

2. *For the cocktail:* In a large pitcher, mix together the remaining ingredients with the cooled simple syrup. It's best to let it chill for a few hours for the flavors to come together, but it's still great right away.

3. Serve over ice.

One of my favorite tricks is infusing simple syrup with herbs like thyme, basil, or mint that I have on hand. All it takes is steeping the herbs for 15 minutes, yet it adds complexity to even the simplest of drinks.

Black Plum and Hibiscus "Sangria"

Sangria is one of my go-to party drinks, something I have made for years. I always have the traditional, alcoholic version and make a nonalcoholic one for those teetotalers and kids. I decided my original nonalcoholic version (basically the sangria juice mix without wine) actually tasted nothing like sangria, and so I set out to make a more tasty adaptation. This one uses fresh black plums and dried hibiscus and is really complex and flavorful with the perfect balance of tart and sweet. VEGAN, GLUTEN-FREE

SERVES 8–10 (YIELDS APPROXIMATELY 9½–10 CUPS)

10 cups water

1¼ cups sugar

1 pound black plums (5–6 plums)

1 cup dried hibiscus flowers

2 cups sliced or chopped fruit: apples, oranges, blackberries, pomegranate arils

mint, for garnish

1. Bring the water, sugar, plums, and hibiscus up to a boil in a large pot. Lower to a simmer and simmer covered for 15 minutes, breaking up the plums every now and then with a wooden spoon. Let cool before handling.

2. Strain through a cheesecloth-lined strainer, squeezing through as much juice as possible. Add the chopped fruit and refrigerate until cool.

3. Serve by itself or over ice with some mint to garnish.

Kahawa in Dar Es Salaam

I could sit and listen all day to my Dad's stories of growing up. He was born and raised in Dar es Salaam, Tanzania's largest city and one that sits on a harbor on the Eastern coast of Africa. The country's history is varied, with it being the center for the Arab slave trade, followed by German and then British rule, and finally independence under Julius Nyerere. The national language of the country is Swahili, but more than 100 different tribal languages are spoken as well as French, Portuguese, and several Indian languages.

His stories always begin when he was around six or seven years old. He'd run home from school in his uniform to play dominos in the afternoon and snack on *nyama choma*, basically East African barbecued meats, for the equivalent of ten cents a piece.

The street food game was serious! Vendors, called *machingas*, would be out on the roadsides, sitting on their straw mats, tempting passersby with the wafting scents of their dishes. Hot corn off the grill, fresh goat meat kebabs, green mangoes with salt and chili, roasted peanuts in Coca Cola, and young coconut boiled with potato were just some of the enticements.

But one (food) story always catches my attention, the kahawa machinga. In Zanzibar, a set of islands that are part of Tanzania, there's a tradition of brewing coffee with spices that dates back to the times of the Arab traders. They call it *Kahawa na Tangawizi* (see my recipe on the next page), which loosely translates to "coffee with ginger."

In Dar es Salaam, the kahawa machinga would walk through the streets clanging his ceramic cups and carrying his brass samovar full of the piping hot coffee. The scent of the spices—cinnamon, cardamom, and ginger—intermingled with the hot strong coffee would bring people out of their homes to get their daily fix.

I'll admit I grew up eating a lot of East African dishes, and some of the foods of his youth are not the easiest to translate, with ingredients that are hard to find and complex preparations. So I truly love to share these simple ones that represent just a little adjustment to the familiar . . . .

Kahawa na Tangawizi (Coffee with Ginger)

This recipe is an inspiration from the East African kahawa guys—a coffee aromatic with cinnamon, cardamom, and ginger that can be done right on the stovetop.

VEGAN, GLUTEN-FREE

SERVES 8–10

2 cups water

¾ teaspoon ground cinnamon

1 teaspoon ground cardamom

1 teaspoon ground ginger

4 tablespoons finely ground coffee

sugar, to taste

1. In a saucepan, bring water with spices up to a boil. Add the ground coffee and bring back up to a boil—it should foam and bubble up to the surface. Remove from the heat until the bubbles subside and then repeat this another two times.

2. Remove from the heat, cover, and let sit 5 minutes. Strain, if desired.

3. Serve hot in espresso cups.

Standard U.S./Metric Measurement Conversions

VOLUME CONVERSIONS

U.S. Volume Measure	Metric Equivalent
⅛ teaspoon	0.5 milliliter
¼ teaspoon	1 milliliter
½ teaspoon	2 milliliters
1 teaspoon	5 milliliters
½ tablespoon	7 milliliters
1 tablespoon (3 teaspoons)	15 milliliters
2 tablespoons (1 fluid ounce)	30 milliliters
¼ cup (4 tablespoons)	60 milliliters
⅓ cup	90 milliliters
½ cup (4 fluid ounces)	125 milliliters
⅔ cup	160 milliliters
¾ cup (6 fluid ounces)	180 milliliters
1 cup (16 tablespoons)	250 milliliters
1 pint (2 cups)	500 milliliters
1 quart (4 cups)	1 liter (about)

WEIGHT CONVERSIONS

U.S. Weight Measure	Metric Equivalent
½ ounce	15 grams
1 ounce	30 grams
2 ounces	60 grams
3 ounces	85 grams
¼ pound (4 ounces)	115 grams
½ pound (8 ounces)	225 grams
¾ pound (12 ounces)	340 grams
1 pound (16 ounces)	454 grams

OVEN TEMPERATURE CONVERSIONS

Degrees Fahrenheit	Degrees Celsius
200 degrees F	95 degrees C
250 degrees F	120 degrees C
275 degrees F	135 degrees C
300 degrees F	150 degrees C
325 degrees F	160 degrees C
350 degrees F	180 degrees C
375 degrees F	190 degrees C
400 degrees F	205 degrees C
425 degrees F	220 degrees C
450 degrees F	230 degrees C

BAKING PAN SIZES

U.S.	Metric
8 × 1½ inch round baking pan	20 × 4 cm cake tin
9 × 1½ inch round baking pan	23 × 3.5 cm cake tin
11 × 7 × 1½ inch baking pan	28 × 18 × 4 cm baking tin
13 × 9 × 2 inch baking pan	30 × 20 × 5 cm baking tin
2 quart rectangular baking dish	30 × 20 × 3 cm baking tin
15 × 10 × 2 inch baking pan	30 × 25 × 2 cm baking tin (Swiss roll tin)
9 inch pie plate	22 × 4 or 23 × 4 cm pie plate
7 or 8 inch springform pan	18 or 20 cm springform or loose bottom cake tin
9 × 5 × 3 inch loaf pan	23 × 13 × 7 cm or 2 lb narrow loaf or pâté tin
1½ quart casserole	1.5 liter casserole
2 quart casserole	2 liter casserole

INDEX

Agrodolce, 288

Aioli, 202–3

Aji amarillo chilies, 34

Ajwain seeds, 13

Alcohol. *See* Drinks

Aleppo chili flakes, 13

Allioli, Catalan, 202–3

Anardana, 13

Arroz Con Pato, 122–25

Art of the Easy Homemade, 70–71

Avocados

    Butter Lettuce Salad with Radish, Avocado, and
Creamy Sesame-Buttermilk Dressing, 86

    Cucumber and Avocado Salad with Yuzu-Honey
Dressing, 78–80

Baked Chicken with Chorizo, Fennel, and Green Olives,
142–43

Balsamic Caramel, 286–88

Balsamic–Red Onion Marmalade, 162–63

Banana Chocolate Chip Muffins, 238–39

BBQ, universal, 144–45

Beans and other legumes

    about: canned chickpeas, 62; fava bean selection and
preparation, 83; peas and rice, 213, 215

    Crispy Roasted Chickpeas with Merkén, Garlic, and
Thyme, 52

    Gran's Peas and Rice, 215–17

    Peruvian Fava Bean and Corn Salad (Solterito), 83

    Red Lentil Paté with Toasted Cashews and Indian
Spices, 49–51

Béchamel and Pasta, 190–92

Beef

    about: making browning, 165

    Cowboy Steak with Tellicherry Peppercorns and
Balsamic–Red Onion Marmalade, 162–63

    Greek Lasagna, 190–92

    Pappardelle with West Indian Stewed Oxtail Ragu,
166–68

    Roasted Marrow Bones with Garlic and Herbed Bread
Crumbs, 176–78

    Rosy's Beef and Potato Patties, 183–85

    Short Rib Chili with Ethiopian Spices, 174–75

    South African Shepherd's Pie (Bobotie), 180–82

Beet greens, garlicky with fish sauce and chili, 210–12

Berbere, 13

Berries

    about: cape gooseberries, 292

    Cape Gooseberry Sour, 291–92

    End-of-Summer Bread Pudding (of sorts), 254–56

    Shrikhand with Strawberries and Balsamic Caramel,
286–88

    South African Milk Tart with Fruits, 277–80

Beverages. *See* Drinks

Biscuits, chicken and, 138–41

Black pepper, 13

Black Plum and Hibiscus "Sangria," 304–5

Bobotie (South African Shepherd's Pie), 180–82

Book overview, 9–10

Brazil, wandering, 91

Bread pudding (of sorts), 254–56

Breads. *See* Biscuits, chicken and; Breakfast, savory tarts,
and breads

Breakfast, savory tarts, and breads, 223–52

    about: beauty of Sunday cooking and eating, 234;
overview of recipes, 223

    Banana Chocolate Chip Muffins, 238–39

    Crab Kedgeree, 232–33

    East African Donuts (Mandazis), 235–37

    Fried "PB&J's," 250–52

    Goat Cheese Tart with Mission Figs, Pistachios, and
Anise, 242–44

    Guava and Cheese Danishes, 245–46

    Mexican Breakfast Quiche, 228–29

    Mushroom and Ajwain Pissaladière, 240–41

    Parker House Rolls with Sweet Miso Butter, 247–49

    Shakshouka with Chorizo and Bread Crumbs, 224–27

    Vanilla-Cinnamon Chia Pudding Parfait, 230–31

Brigadeiros, espresso-chocolate, 281–83

Browning, making, 165

Butter

    about: 15; browning, 219

    Green Chili Butter, 194

    Sweet Miso Butter, 247–48

Butterflied Za'atar Roast Chicken, 118–21

Butter Lettuce Salad with Radish, Avocado, and Creamy
Sesame-Buttermilk Dressing, 86

Cakes
    Hot Coffee-Glazed Medjool Date Cakes, 263–65
    Mexican Chocolate Loaf Cake, 260–62
    Nani's Fruit Spice Cake, 274–76
Calamari, sautéed, 88–90
Cantaloupe, in Melon Horchata, 293–94
Cape Gooseberry Sour, 291–92
Caramel, balsamic, 286–88
Caramel, for Persimmon Tarte Tatin, 257–58
Caramels, salted with sweet garam masala, 270–71
Cardamom, 13, 173, 237
Carrots, in Green Mango and Carrot Slaw with Fresh
    Chili, Peanuts, and Mint, 85
Cassava, 15
Cassava Fries with Chili-Lime Salt, 222
Cast-iron skillets, 17
Catalan Allioli, 202–3
Cauliflower, roasted with bread crumbs, saffron, and dried
    cranberries, 199–201
Chai-Spiced Sweet Potato Pie, 220–21
Champagne floaters, 300
Charred Honey-Miso Smoked Salmon, 96–97
Cheddar-Parm Crackers with Ajwain and Truffle Oil,
    37–38
Cheese
    about: homemade, making quickly, 70–71
    Cheddar-Parm Crackers with Ajwain and Truffle Oil,
        37–38
    Exotic Cheese Crackers, 36–38
    Goat Cheese Tart with Mission Figs, Pistachios, and
        Anise, 242–44
    Guava and Cheese Danishes, 245–46
    Harissa and Cheese–Stuffed Fried Olives, 30–32
    Heirloom Tomato Galettes with Urfa Chilies, Mint,
        and Ricotta Salata, 41–43
    Manchego Cheese Crackers with Anardana, 37–38
    Massaged Kale Salad with Pear, Fresh Cheese, and
        Pomegranate Vinaigrette, 72–74
    Pepper Jack Crackers with Garlic and Herbs, 38
Chermoula, 109–10
Cherries
    about: ground, cape gooseberries as, 292
    Cherry-Yuzu Champagne Floaters, 300
    Meyer Lemon Cream with "Amarena-Style" Cherries,
        267–69
Chestnut soup, spiced, 66–67
Chia seeds
    about, 15; nutritional benefits, 15, 231
    Vanilla-Cinnamon Chia Pudding Parfait, 230–31
Chicken. See Poultry

Chicken Fried Scallops, 98–99
Chickpeas
    about: using canned, 62
    Crispy Roasted Chickpeas with Merkén, Garlic, and
        Thyme, 52
    Harira, 61–62
Chilies, 15–16, 17, 34, 81
Chili flakes, Aleppo, 13
Chili flakes, Urfa, 15
Chili-Lime Salt, 222
Chili powder, 13
Chili seasoning recipes
    Harissa, 21, 24
    Merkén, 24
    Sambal Oelek, 25
Chipotle Glaze, 154–56
Chocolate
    about: Dutch process cocoa powder, 16, 262; Mexican,
        16
    Banana Chocolate Chip Muffins, 238–39
    Espresso-Chocolate Brigadeiros, 281–83
    Mexican Chocolate Loaf Cake, 260–62
Chorizo. See Sausage (chorizo)
Citrus
    about: orange blossom water, 17
    Chili-Lime Salt, 222
    Frozen Limonada, 295
    Israeli Couscous Salad with Lemon, Fennel, and Basil,
        75–77
    Lemon-Egg Soup with Quinoa, 68–69
    Meyer Lemon Cream with "Amarena-Style" Cherries,
        267–69
    Pink Grapefruit Paloma, 296–97
    Sweet Lemon-Ginger Confit, 151–52
    Thyme-Green Tea Cocktail, 301–3
Clams
    Paella de Marisco, 112–15
    Peruvian Clams à la Parmesana, 33–35
Coconut
    Corn with Green Chili Butter and Toasted Coconut,
        194–95
    Mussels with African Chilies and Coconut (Moqueca-
        Style), 93–95
Coconut milk, 16
Coffee
    Espresso-Chocolate Brigadeiros, 281–83
    Hot Coffee-Glazed Medjool Date Cakes, 263–65
    Kahawa na Tangawizi (Coffee with Ginger), 308
Coffee grinders, 17–18
Confit, sweet lemon-ginger, 151–52

Corn
    Corn with Green Chili Butter and Toasted Coconut, 194–95
    Homemade Popcorn with Spiced Honey and Butter, 56
    Peruvian Fava Bean and Corn Salad (Solterito), 83
    Smoky Corn Pudding with Mustard Seeds and Curry Leaves, 207–9
Cornish hens, Jamaican jerk, 146–47
Couscous salad with lemon, fennel, and basil, 75–77
Cowboy Steak with Tellicherry Peppercorns and Balsamic–Red Onion Marmalade, 162–63
Crab
    Crab Cakes with Mustard Seeds and Parsnips, 107–8
    Crab Kedgeree, 232–33
Crackers
    Cheddar-Parm Crackers with Ajwain and Truffle Oil, 37–38
    Exotic Cheese Crackers, 36–38
    Manchego Cheese Crackers with Anardana, 37–38
    Pepper Jack Crackers with Garlic and Herbs, 38
Creamy Sesame-Buttermilk Dressing, 86
Creole seasoning, NOLA, 26
Creole Shrimp and Grits, 100–101
Crispy, Brick Chicken Thighs with Roasted Garlic and Sweet Lemon-Ginger Confit, 151–52
Crispy Roasted Chickpeas with Merkén, Garlic, and Thyme, 52
Cucumber and Avocado Salad with Yuzu-Honey Dressing, 78–80
Curry leaves, 16

Danishes, guava and cheese, 245–46
Dates
    about: Medjool, 16, 264
    Hot Coffee-Glazed Medjool Date Cakes, 263–65
Desserts, 253–88
    about: Grandmother's Tribute, 272–73; overview of recipes, 253
    End-of-Summer Bread Pudding (of sorts), 254–56
    Espresso-Chocolate Brigadeiros, 281–83
    Hibiscus Paletas, 284–85
    Hot Coffee-Glazed Medjool Date Cakes, 263–65
    Mexican Chocolate Loaf Cake, 260–62
    Meyer Lemon Cream with "Amarena-Style" Cherries, 267–69
    Nani's Fruit Spice Cake, 274–76
    Persimmon Tarte Tatin, 257–59
    Salted Caramels with Sweet Garam Masala, 270–71
    Shrikhand with Strawberries and Balsamic Caramel, 286–88

South African Milk Tart with Fruits, 277–80
Deviled Eggs Three Ways: Indonesian, Greek, and Mexican, 46–48
Dill seeds, 14
Dip, smoky eggplant with fingerling chips, 53–55
Donuts, East African (Mandazis), 235–37
Dressings. *See* Sauces, dressings, marinades, etc.
Drinks, 289–308
    about: infusing simple syrup with herbs, 302; overview of recipes, 289
    Black Plum and Hibiscus "Sangria," 304–5
    Cape Gooseberry Sour, 291–92
    Cherry-Yuzu Champagne Floaters, 300
    Frozen Limonada, 295
    Kahawa na Tangawizi (Coffee with Ginger), 308
    Melon Horchata, 293–94
    Pink Grapefruit Paloma, 296–97
    St. Lucian Rum Punch, 298–99
    Thyme-Green Tea Cocktail, 301–3
Dukkah, Egyptian, 20–21
Dutch ovens, 18
Dutch process cocoa powder, 16, 262

East African Donuts (Mandazis), 235–37
Eggplant, in Smoky Eggplant Dip with Fingerling Chips, 53–55
Eggs
    Deviled Eggs Three Ways: Indonesian, Greek, and Mexican, 46–48
    Lemon-Egg Soup with Quinoa, 68–69
    Mexican Breakfast Quiche, 228–29
    Shakshouka with Chorizo and Bread Crumbs, 224–27
Egyptian Dukkah, 20–21
End-of-Summer Bread Pudding (of sorts), 254–56
Equipment, 17–18
Espresso-Chipotle St Louis–Style Spare Ribs, 154–56
Espresso-Chocolate Brigadeiros, 281–83
Exotic Cheese Crackers, 36–38

Fats, 15
Feijoada, 160–61
Fennel
    Baked Chicken with Chorizo, Fennel, and Green Olives, 142–43
    Israeli Couscous Salad with Lemon, Fennel, and Basil, 75–77
Fenugreek, 14
Figs, in Goat Cheese Tart with Mission Figs, Pistachios, and Anise, 242–44

Fish and seafood, 87–116
  about: overview of recipes, 87; Peruvian options, 81;
    preparing mussels, 94; in Turkey, 39
  Charred Honey-Miso Smoked Salmon, 96–97
  Chicken Fried Scallops, 98–99
  Crab Cakes with Mustard Seeds and Parsnips, 107–8
  Crab Kedgeree, 232–33
  Creole Shrimp and Grits, 100–101
  Lobster Macaroni Pie with Bacon Bread Crumbs, 104–5
  Mussels with African Chilies and Coconut (Moqueca-
    Style), 93–95
  Paella de Marisco, 112–15
  Peruvian Clams à la Parmesana, 33–35
  Salt-Baked Fish with Chermoula, 109–11
  Sautéed Rhode Island Calamari with Garlic, Cherry
    Peppers, and Bread Crumbs, 88–90
  Tiradito with "Leche de Tigre," 116
Food Is Giving, 266
Fried "PB&J's," 250–52
Frozen Limonada, 295
Fruit
  Chicken Salad with Bacon, Walnuts, and Fruit, 133–34
  drinks with. See Drinks
  Nani's Fruit Spice Cake, 274–76
  South African Milk Tart with Fruits, 277–80
Fruit molasses
  about, 16
  Homemade Pomegranate Molasses, 19–20

Galettes, heirloom tomato with Urfa chilies, mint, and
  ricotta salata, 41–43
Garam masala, 14
Garlic
  about: granulated, 14
  Garlicky Beet Greens with Fish Sauce and Chili,
    210–12
  Roasted Garlic, 26
Ginger
  Kahawa na Tangawizi (Coffee with Ginger), 308
  Sweet Lemon-Ginger Confit, 151–52
Gluten-free recipes
  Black Plum and Hibiscus "Sangria," 304–5
  Butterflied Za'atar Roast Chicken, 118–21
  Cassava Fries with Chili-Lime Salt, 222
  Cherry-Yuzu Champagne Floaters, 300
  Corn with Green Chili Butter and Toasted Coconut,
    194–95
  Crab Kedgeree, 232–33
  Crispy, Brick Chicken Thighs with Roasted Garlic and
    Sweet Lemon-Ginger Confit, 151–52

Crispy Roasted Chickpeas with Merkén, Garlic, and
  Thyme, 52
Deviled Eggs Three Ways: Indonesian, Greek, and
  Mexican, 46–48
Egyptian Dukkah, 20–21
Espresso-Chipotle St Louis–Style Spare Ribs, 154–56
Espresso-Chocolate Brigadeiros, 281–83
Frozen Limonada, 295
Gran's Peas and Rice, 215–17
Green Mango and Carrot Slaw with Fresh Chili,
  Peanuts, and Mint, 85
Harira, 61–62
Harissa, 21, 24
Hibiscus Paletas, 284–85
Homemade Pomegranate Molasses, 19–20
Homemade Popcorn with Spiced Honey and Butter, 56
Honey-Braised Lamb Shanks with Butternut Squash
  and Apples, 157–59
Kahawa na Tangawizi (Coffee with Ginger), 308
Kenyan Coconut-Coriander Chicken, 126–27
Lemon-Egg Soup with Quinoa, 68–69
Massaged Kale Salad with Pear, Fresh Cheese, and
  Pomegranate Vinaigrette, 72–74
Melon Horchata, 293–94
Merkén, 24
Meyer Lemon Cream with "Amarena-Style" Cherries,
  267–69
My Feijoada, 160–61
NOLA Creole Seasoning, 25–26
Peruvian Fava Bean and Corn Salad (Solterito), 83
Roasted Garlic, 26
Salt-Baked Fish with Chermoula, 109–11
Salted Caramels with Sweet Garam Masala, 270–71
Sambal Oelek, 25
Shrikhand with Strawberries and Balsamic Caramel,
  286–88
Smoky Eggplant Dip with Fingerling Chips, 53–55
Sopa de Flor de Calabaza (Squash Blossom Soup),
  58–60
Spiced Chestnut Soup, 66–67
Spiced Honey, 28
St. Lucian Rum Punch, 298–99
Sugar and Spice Pecans, 44–45
Summer Squash and Burst Cherry Tomatoes with
  Brown Butter, Coriander, and Hazelnuts Chai-,
  218–19
Thyme-Green Tea Cocktail, 301–3
Tiradito with "Leche de Tigre," 116
Vanilla-Cinnamon Chia Pudding Parfait, 230–31
West African Tsire, 27–28
Za'atar, 27

Goat Biryani, 186–89
Goat Cheese Tart with Mission Figs, Pistachios, and Anise, 242–44
Gooseberries, in Cape Gooseberry Sour, 291–92
Grandmother, tribute to, 272–73
Greek-inspired deviled eggs, 46–48
Green Mango and Carrot Slaw with Fresh Chili, Peanuts, and Mint, 85
Greens. *See also* Salads
    about: washing, 210–12
    Garlicky Beet Greens with Fish Sauce and Chili, 210–12
Grits, Creole shrimp and, 100–101
Guava and Cheese Danishes, 245–46
Guava paste, 16

Harira, 61–62
Harissa, 21, 24
Harissa and Cheese–Stuffed Fried Olives, 30–32
Heirloom Tomato Galettes with Urfa Chilies, Mint, and Ricotta Salata, 41–43
Hibiscus flowers (dried)
    about, 16
    Black Plum and Hibiscus "Sangria," 304–5
    Hibiscus Paletas, 284–85
Homemade, ease of making, 70–71
Homemade Pomegranate Molasses, 19–20
Homemade Popcorn with Spiced Honey and Butter, 56
Honey, Spiced, 28
Horchata, melon, 293–94
Hors d'oeuvres and snacks, 29–56
    about: overview of recipes, 29
    Cheddar-Parm Crackers with Ajwain and Truffle Oil, 37–38
    Crispy Roasted Chickpeas with Merkén, Garlic, and Thyme, 52
    Deviled Eggs Three Ways: Indonesian, Greek, and Mexican, 46–48
    Exotic Cheese Crackers, 36–38
    Harissa and Cheese–Stuffed Fried Olives, 30–32
    Heirloom Tomato Galettes with Urfa Chilies, Mint, and Ricotta Salata, 41–43
    Homemade Popcorn with Spiced Honey and Butter, 56
    Manchego Cheese Crackers with Anardana, 37–38
    Pepper Jack Crackers with Garlic and Herbs, 38
    Peruvian Clams à la Parmesana, 33–35
    Red Lentil Paté with Toasted Cashews and Indian Spices, 49–51
    Smoky Eggplant Dip with Fingerling Chips, 53–55
    Sugar and Spice Pecans, 44–45
Hot Coffee-Glazed Medjool Date Cakes, 263–65

Ice cream scoops, 18
Indonesian-inspired deviled eggs, 46–48
Ingredients. *See also specific main ingredients*
    about: overview of, 11
    cooking guidelines, 15
    fats, 15
    gluten-free. *See* Gluten-free recipes
    importance of, 204
    select ones used in book, list of, 15–17
    spices, 12–15. *See also specific spices*
    vegan. *See* Vegan recipes
    vegetarian. *See* Vegetarian recipes
    where to buy, 18–19
Israeli Couscous Salad with Lemon, Fennel, and Basil, 75–77

Jamaican Jerk Hens, 146–47
Japanese mandolines, 18

Kahawa in Dar Es Salaam, 307
Kahawa na Tangawizi (Coffee with Ginger), 308
Kale, in Massaged Kale Salad with Pear, Fresh Cheese, and Pomegranate Vinaigrette, 72–74
Kenyan Coconut-Coriander Chicken, 126–27
Kitchen equipment, 17–18
Korean-Style BBQ Chicken or Turkey Drumsticks, 135–37

Lamb
    Honey-Braised Lamb Shanks with Butternut Squash and Apples, 157–59
    Smoky Lamb Meatballs, 172–73
"Leche de Tigre," 116
Lemon. *See* Citrus
Lentils
    Harira, 61–62
    Red Lentil Paté with Toasted Cashews and Indian Spices, 49–51
Lobster Macaroni Pie with Bacon Bread Crumbs, 104–5

Manchego Cheese Crackers with Anardana, 37–38
Mandazis (East African Donuts), 235–37
Mandolines, Japanese, 18
Mangoes, in Green Mango and Carrot Slaw with Fresh Chili, Peanuts, and Mint, 85
Marrow bones, roasted, 176–78
Martinis. *See* Cape Gooseberry Sour
Massaged Kale Salad with Pear, Fresh Cheese, and Pomegranate Vinaigrette, 72–74

Measurement conversion charts, 309
Meatballs, smoky lamb, 172–73
Meat dishes, 153–92
    about: making browning, 165; overview of recipes, 153
    Cowboy Steak with Tellicherry Peppercorns and
        Balsamic–Red Onion Marmalade, 162–63
    Espresso-Chipotle St Louis–Style Spare Ribs, 154–56
    Goat Biryani, 186–89
    Greek Lasagna, 190–92
    Honey-Braised Lamb Shanks with Butternut Squash
        and Apples, 157–59
    My Feijoada, 160–61
    Pappardelle with West Indian Stewed Oxtail Ragu,
        166–68
    Pork Chops with West African Tsire and Pan Gravy,
        169–71
    Roasted Marrow Bones with Garlic and Herbed Bread
        Crumbs, 176–78
    Rosy's Beef and Potato Patties, 183–85
    Short Rib Chili with Ethiopian Spices, 174–75
    Smoky Lamb Meatballs, 172–73
    South African Shepherd's Pie (Bobotie), 180–82
Medjool dates. See Dates
Melktart (South African milk tart), 277–80
Melon Horchata, 293–94
Merkén, 24
Metric conversions, 309
Mexican Breakfast Quiche, 228–29
Mexican chocolate, 16
Mexican Chocolate Loaf Cake, 260–62
Mexican drinks. See Drinks
Mexican-inspired deviled eggs, 46–48
Meyer Lemon Cream with "Amarena-Style" Cherries,
    267–69
Milk tart with fruits, South African, 277–80
Mirin, 16
Miso butter, sweet, 247–48
Miso paste, 16–17
Mixers, stand, 18
Molasses, fruit. See Fruit molasses
Moroccan Chicken Pie, 149–50
Moroccan curry. See Ras El Hanout
Moroccan soup. See Harira
Mushrooms
    about: types of, 241
    Mushroom and Ajwain Pissaladière, 240–41
    Wild Mushroom Quinotto, 196–98
Mussels
    Mussels with African Chilies and Coconut (Moqueca-
        Style), 93–95
    Paella de Marisco, 112–15

Mustard seeds, 14
My Feijoada, 160–61

Nani's Fruit Spice Cake, 274–76
Nigella seeds, 14
NOLA Creole Seasoning, 25–26
Nuts and seeds
    about: chia seeds, 15; toasting walnuts, 134
    Chicken Salad with Bacon, Walnuts, and Fruit, 133–34
    Fried "PB&J's," 250–52
    Goat Cheese Tart with Mission Figs, Pistachios, and
        Anise, 242–44
    Green Mango and Carrot Slaw with Fresh Chili,
        Peanuts, and Mint, 85
    Red Lentil Paté with Toasted Cashews and Indian
        Spices, 49–51
    Spiced Chestnut Soup, 66–67
    Sugar and Spice Pecans, 44–45
    Summer Squash and Burst Cherry Tomatoes with
        Brown Butter, Coriander, and Hazelnuts Chai-,
        218–19
    Vanilla-Cinnamon Chia Pudding Parfait, 230–31
Za'atar, 27

Oils, 15
Olives, harissa and cheese–stuffed fried, 30–32
Onion
    about: granulated, 14
    Balsamic–Red Onion Marmalade, 162–63
Orange blossom water, 17
Oxtail ragu, West Indian stewed, 166–68

Paella de Marisco, 112–15
Palate, importance of, 18
Paletas, hibiscus, 284–85
Palm sugar, 17
Pappardelle with West Indian Stewed Oxtail Ragu, 166–68
Paprika, smoked Spanish (Pimentón de La Vera), 14
Parker House Rolls with Sweet Miso Butter, 247–49
Parsnips
    Crab Cakes with Mustard Seeds and Parsnips, 107–8
    Savory Winter Vegetable Crumble, 205–6
Pasta
    Béchamel and Pasta, 190–92
    Greek Lasagna, 190–92
    Lobster Macaroni Pie with Bacon Bread Crumbs, 104–5
Pastries and such. See Breakfast, savory tarts, and breads;
    Desserts

Patatas Bravas–Inspired Salad, 202–3

"PB&J's," fried, 250–52

Pears, in Massaged Kale Salad with Pear, Fresh Cheese, and
Pomegranate Vinaigrette, 72–74

Pepper, black, 13

Pepper Jack Crackers with Garlic and Herbs, 38

Peppers
about: chilies, 15–16, 17, 34, 81; removing before
bursting, 213; Scotch bonnet, 213
Harissa, 21, 24

Persimmon Tarte Tatin, 257–59

Peruvian chilies, 17

Peruvian Clams à la Parmesana, 33–35

Peruvian Fava Bean and Corn Salad (Solterito), 83

Peruvian Rhythms, 81–82

Pies, savory
Chai-Spiced Sweet Potato Pie, 220–21
Lobster Macaroni Pie with Bacon Bread Crumbs, 104–5
Moroccan Chicken Pie, 149–50
South African Shepherd's Pie (Bobotie), 180–82

Pimentón de La Vera (smoked Spanish paprika), 14

Pink Grapefruit Paloma, 296–97

Pissaladière, mushroom and, 240–41

Pomegranate
Homemade Pomegranate Molasses, 19–20
Pomegranate Vinaigrette, 72–74

Popcorn with spiced honey and butter, 56

Pork. See also Sausage (chorizo)
Espresso-Chipotle St Louis–Style Spare Ribs, 154–56
My Feijoada, 160–61
Pork Chops with West African Tsire and Pan Gravy,
169–71
South African Shepherd's Pie (Bobotie), 180–82
Trinidadian-Chinese Wonton Soup, 63–65

Potatoes
Patatas Bravas–Inspired Salad, 202–3
Rosy's Beef and Potato Patties, 183–85
Smoky Eggplant Dip with Fingerling Chips, 53–55

Potato ricers, 18

Poultry, 117–52
about: frying chicken (step-by-step), 128–29; overview
of recipes, 117; Thanksgiving mashup, 102; universal
BBQ, 144–45
Arroz Con Pato, 122–25
Baked Chicken with Chorizo, Fennel, and Green
Olives, 142–43
Butterflied Za'atar Roast Chicken, 118–21
"Chicken and Biscuits," 138–41
Chicken Salad with Bacon, Walnuts, and Fruit, 133–34
Crispy, Brick Chicken Thighs with Roasted Garlic and
Sweet Lemon-Ginger Confit, 151–52

Jamaican Jerk Hens, 146–47

Kenyan Coconut-Coriander Chicken, 126–27

Korean-Style BBQ Chicken or Turkey Drumsticks,
135–37

Moroccan Chicken Pie, 149–50

Saffron Fried Chicken, 130–32

Puddings
End-of-Summer Bread Pudding (of sorts), 254–56
Smoky Corn Pudding with Mustard Seeds and Curry
Leaves, 207–9
Vanilla-Cinnamon Chia Pudding Parfait, 230–31

Quinoa
Lemon-Egg Soup with Quinoa, 68–69
Wild Mushroom Quinotto, 196–98

Ras El Hanout, 25, 45

Red Lentil Paté with Toasted Cashews and Indian Spices,
49–51

Ribs. See Meat dishes

Rice
about: paella, 17; peas and, 213, 215
Arroz Con Pato, 122–25
Gran's Peas and Rice, 215–17
Paella de Marisco, 112–14

Roasted Cauliflower with Bread Crumbs, Saffron, and
Dried Cranberries, 199–201

Roasted Garlic, 26

Roasted Marrow Bones with Garlic and Herbed Bread
Crumbs, 176–78

Rosy's Beef and Potato Patties, 183–85

Rum punch, St. Lucian, 298–99

Saffron, 14

Saffron Fried Chicken, 130–32

Salads
about: overview of recipes, 57
Butter Lettuce Salad with Radish, Avocado, and
Creamy Sesame-Buttermilk Dressing, 86
Chicken Salad with Bacon, Walnuts, and Fruit, 133–34
Cucumber and Avocado Salad with Yuzu-Honey
Dressing, 78–80
Green Mango and Carrot Slaw with Fresh Chili,
Peanuts, and Mint, 85
Israeli Couscous Salad with Lemon, Fennel, and Basil,
75–77
Massaged Kale Salad with Pear, Fresh Cheese, and
Pomegranate Vinaigrette, 72–74

Patatas Bravas–Inspired Salad, 202–3
Peruvian Fava Bean and Corn Salad (Solterito), 83
Salmon, charred honey-miso smoked, 96–97
Salt
    about, 12–13
    Chili-Lime Salt, 222
Salt-Baked Fish with Chermoula, 109–11
Salted Caramels with Sweet Garam Masala, 270–71
Sambal Oelek, 25
"Sangria," black plum and hibiscus, 304–5
Sauces, dressings, marinades, etc.
    about: making browning, 165; stocks, 17
    Balsamic–Red Onion Marmalade, 162–63
    Béchamel and Pasta, 190–92
    Catalan Allioli, 202–3
    Chermoula, 109–10
    Chipotle Glaze, 154–56
    Creamy Sesame-Buttermilk Dressing, 86
    "Leche de Tigre," 116
    Pomegranate Vinaigrette, 72–74
    Sweet Lemon-Ginger Confit, 151–52
    West African Tsire and Pan Gravy, 169–71
    Yuzu-Honey Dressing, 78–80
Sauces, sweet
    Apricot Glaze, 274–76
    Balsamic Caramel, 286–88
    Caramel, 257–58
Sausage (chorizo)
    Baked Chicken with Chorizo, Fennel, and Green
        Olives, 142–43
    My Feijoada, 160–61
    Paella de Marisco, 112–14
    Shakshouka with Chorizo and Bread Crumbs, 224–27
Sautéed Rhode Island Calamari with Garlic, Cherry
    Peppers, and Bread Crumbs, 88–90
Savory Winter Vegetable Crumble, 205–6
Scallops, chicken fried, 98–99
Shakshouka with Chorizo and Bread Crumbs, 224–27
Short Rib Chili with Ethiopian Spices, 174–75
Shrikhand with Strawberries and Balsamic Caramel,
    286–88
Shrimp
    Creole Shrimp and Grits, 100–101
    Paella de Marisco, 112–14
Side dishes. See Vegetables and side dishes
Skillets, cast-iron, 17
Smoky Corn Pudding with Mustard Seeds and Curry
    Leaves, 207–9
Smoky Eggplant Dip with Fingerling Chips, 53–55
Smoky Lamb Meatballs, 172–73
Snacks. See Hors d'oeuvres and snacks

Solterito (Peruvian Fava Bean and Corn Salad), 83
Sopa de Flor de Calabaza (Squash Blossom Soup), 58–60
Soups and stews
    about: overview of recipes, 57; stocks, 17
    Harira, 61–62
    Lemon-Egg Soup with Quinoa, 68–69
    Pappardelle with West Indian Stewed Oxtail Ragu,
        166–68
    Short Rib Chili with Ethiopian Spices, 174–75
    Sopa de Flor de Calabaza (Squash Blossom Soup),
        58–60
    Spiced Chestnut Soup, 66–67
    Trinidadian-Chinese Wonton Soup, 63–65
South African cookery, lesson in, 179
South African Milk Tart with Fruits, 277–80
South African Shepherd's Pie (Bobotie), 180–82
Spice cake, 274–76
Spiced Chestnut Soup, 66–67
Spiced Honey, 28
Spices. See also specific spices
    author's personal trade, 22
    commonly used in this book, 12–15
    hot, types of, 13
    keeping fresh, 12
    measuring, 12
    storing, 12
    toasting, 12, 20
    whole vs. ground, 12
Spice/seasoning recipes
    Egyptian Dukkah, 20–21
    Harissa, 21, 24
    Merkén, 24
    NOLA Creole Seasoning, 25–26
    Ras El Hanout, 25, 45
    Roasted Garlic, 26
    Sambal Oelek, 25
    West African Tsire, 27–28
    Za'atar, 27
Squash
    Honey-Braised Lamb Shanks with Butternut Squash
        and Apples, 157–59
    Savory Winter Vegetable Crumble, 205–6
    Sopa de Flor de Calabaza (Squash Blossom Soup),
        58–60
    Summer Squash and Burst Cherry Tomatoes with
        Brown Butter, Coriander, and Hazelnuts   Chai-,
        218–19
Squid. See Sautéed Rhode Island Calamari with Garlic,
    Cherry Peppers, and Bread Crumbs
Stand mixers, 18
St. Lucian Rum Punch, 298–99

Stocks, about, 17
Stories
  Art of the Easy Homemade, 70–71
  Beauty of Sunday Cooking and Eating, 234
  Don't Let the Pepper Burst!, 213
  Food Is Giving, 266
  Grandmother's Tribute, 272–73
  How to Make Browning, 165
  Importance of Ingredients, 204
  Kahawa in Dar Es Salaam, 307
  A Lesson in South African Cookery, 179
  My Personal Spice Trade, 22
  My Thanksgiving Mashup, 102
  Peruvian Rhythms, 81–82
  Turkey's Culinary Crossroads, 39–40
  Universal BBQ, 144–45
  Virtue of Fried Chicken (steps to fried chicken
    nirvana), 128–29
  Wandering Brazil, 91
Storing spices, 12
Strawberries. *See* Berries
Sugar, palm, 17
Sugar and Spice Pecans, 44–45
Sumac, 14
Summer Squash and Burst Cherry Tomatoes with Brown
  Butter, Coriander, and Hazelnuts Chai-, 218–19
Sunday, beauty of cooking/eating on, 234
Sweet Lemon-Ginger Confit, 151–52
Sweet Miso Butter, 247–48
Sweet potatoes
  Chai-Spiced Sweet Potato Pie, 220–21
  Savory Winter Vegetable Crumble, 205–6
Sweets. *See* Desserts; Sauces, sweet

Tandoor, in Turkey, 40
Taramosalata, about, 48
Tarte tatin, persimmon, 257–59
Tarts. *See* Breakfast, savory tarts, and breads; Desserts
Tawa, in Turkey, 40
Tea, in Thyme-Green Tea Cocktail, 301–3
Thanksgiving mashup, 102
Thyme-Green Tea Cocktail, 301–3
Tiradito with "Leche de Tigre," 116
Toasting
  spices, 12, 20
  walnuts, 134
Tomatoes
  Harira, 61–62
  Heirloom Tomato Galettes with Urfa Chilies, Mint,
    and Ricotta Salata, 41–43

Summer Squash and Burst Cherry Tomatoes with
  Brown Butter, Coriander, and Hazelnuts Chai-,
  218–19
Trinidadian-Chinese Wonton Soup, 63–65
Tsire, West African, 27–28
Turkey drumsticks, Korean-style BBQ, 135–37
Turmeric, 15

Vanilla-Cinnamon Chia Pudding Parfait, 230–31
Veal, in South African Shepherd's Pie (Bobotie), 180–82
Vegan recipes
  Black Plum and Hibiscus "Sangria," 304–5
  Cassava Fries with Chili-Lime Salt, 222
  Cherry-Yuzu Champagne Floaters, 300
  Crispy Roasted Chickpeas with Merkén, Garlic, and
    Thyme, 52
  East African Donuts (Mandazis), 235–37
  Egyptian Dukkah, 20–21
  Frozen Limonada, 295
  Green Mango and Carrot Slaw with Fresh Chili,
    Peanuts, and Mint, 85
  Harissa, 21, 24
  Hibiscus Paletas, 284–85
  Homemade Pomegranate Molasses, 19–20
  Israeli Couscous Salad with Lemon, Fennel, and Basil,
    75–77
  Kahawa na Tangawizi (Coffee with Ginger), 308
  Melon Horchata, 293–94
  Merkén, 24
  NOLA Creole Seasoning, 25–26
  Pink Grapefruit Paloma, 296–97
  Ras El Hanout, 25
  Red Lentil Paté with Toasted Cashews and Indian
    Spices, 49–51
  Roasted Garlic, 26
  Sambal Oelek, 25
  St. Lucian Rum Punch, 298–99
  Thyme-Green Tea Cocktail, 301–3
  West African Tsire, 27–28
  Za'atar, 27
Vegetables and side dishes, 193–222. *See also specific
  vegetables*
  about: overview of recipes, 193; roasting vegetables, 200
  Cassava Fries with Chili-Lime Salt, 222
  Chai-Spiced Sweet Potato Pie, 220–21
  Corn with Green Chili Butter and Toasted Coconut,
    194–95
  Garlicky Beet Greens with Fish Sauce and Chili,
    210–12
  Gran's Peas and Rice, 215–17

Patatas Bravas–Inspired Salad, 202–3
Roasted Cauliflower with Bread Crumbs, Saffron, and
  Dried Cranberries, 199–201
Savory Winter Vegetable Crumble, 205–6
Smoky Corn Pudding with Mustard Seeds and Curry
  Leaves, 207–9
Summer Squash and Burst Cherry Tomatoes with
  Brown Butter, Coriander, and Hazelnuts   Chai-,
  218–19
Wild Mushroom Quinotto, 196–98
Vegetarian recipes. See also Vegan recipes
Banana Chocolate Chip Muffins, 238–39
Butter Lettuce Salad with Radish, Avocado, and
  Creamy Sesame-Buttermilk Dressing, 86
Cape Gooseberry Sour, 291–92
Chai-Spiced Sweet Potato Pie, 220–21
Cheddar-Parm Crackers with Ajwain and Truffle Oil,
  37–38
Corn with Green Chili Butter and Toasted Coconut,
  194–95
Cucumber and Avocado Salad with Yuzu-Honey
  Dressing, 78–80
Deviled Eggs Three Ways: Indonesian, Greek, and
  Mexican, 46–48
End-of-Summer Bread Pudding (of sorts), 254–56
Espresso-Chocolate Brigadeiros, 281–83
Exotic Cheese Crackers, 36–38
Fried "PB&J's," 250–52
Goat Cheese Tart with Mission Figs, Pistachios, and
  Anise, 242–44
Gran's Peas and Rice (eliminating pork/bacon), 215–17
Guava and Cheese Danishes, 245–46
Harissa and Cheese–Stuffed Fried Olives, 30–32
Heirloom Tomato Galettes with Urfa Chilies, Mint,
  and Ricotta Salata, 41–43
Homemade Popcorn with Spiced Honey and Butter, 56
Hot Coffee-Glazed Medjool Date Cakes, 263–65
Manchego Cheese Crackers with Anardana, 37–38
Massaged Kale Salad with Pear, Fresh Cheese, and
  Pomegranate Vinaigrette, 72–74
Mexican Breakfast Quiche, 228–29
Mexican Chocolate Loaf Cake, 260–62
Meyer Lemon Cream with "Amarena-Style" Cherries,
  267–69
Mushroom and Ajwain Pissaladière, 240–41
Nani's Fruit Spice Cake, 274–76
Parker House Rolls with Sweet Miso Butter, 247–49
Patatas Bravas–Inspired Salad, 202–3
Pepper Jack Crackers with Garlic and Herbs, 38
Persimmon Tarte Tatin, 257–59
Peruvian Fava Bean and Corn Salad (Solterito), 83

Pink Grapefruit Paloma, 296–97
Roasted Cauliflower with Bread Crumbs, Saffron, and
  Dried Cranberries, 199–201
Salted Caramels with Sweet Garam Masala, 270–71
Savory Winter Vegetable Crumble, 205–6
Shrikhand with Strawberries and Balsamic Caramel,
  286–88
Smoky Corn Pudding with Mustard Seeds and Curry
  Leaves, 207–9
Smoky Eggplant Dip with Fingerling Chips, 53–55
Spiced Honey, 28
South African Milk Tart with Fruits, 277–80
Sugar and Spice Pecans, 44–45
Summer Squash and Burst Cherry Tomatoes with
  Brown Butter, Coriander, and Hazelnuts Chai-,
  218–19
Thyme-Green Tea Cocktail, 301–3
Vanilla-Cinnamon Chia Pudding Parfait, 230–31
Wild Mushroom Quinotto, 196–98
Vinaigrette. See Sauces, dressings, marinades, etc.

Water baths, 182
West African Tsire, 27–28
Wild Mushroom Quinotto, 196–98
Wonton soup, Trinidadian-Chinese, 63–65

Yogurt, making Greek, 70
Yuzu
  about, 17; finding at market, 80
  Yuzu-Honey Dressing, 78–80

Za'atar, 27